creating spreadsheets
and charts in
Microsoft Office Excel 2007
for Windows

Visual QuickProject Guide

by Maria Langer

Peachpit
Press

Visual QuickProject Guide

Creating Spreadsheets and Charts
in Microsoft Office Excel 2007 for Windows

Maria Langer

Peachpit Press
1249 Eighth Street
Berkeley, CA 94710
510/524-2178
800/283-9444
510/524-2221 (fax)

Find us on the Web at: www.peachpit.com
To report errors, please send a note to errata@peachpit.com
Peachpit Press is a division of Pearson Education

Copyright © 2007 by Maria Langer

Editor: Nancy Davis
Production Editor: David Van Ness
Proofreader: Tracy O'Connell
Compositor: Maria Langer
Indexer: Julie Bess
Interior design: Elizabeth Castro
Cover design: Peachpit Press, Aren Howell
Cover photo credit: iStockphoto/Anneke Schram

ISBN 0-321-49238-2

9 8 7 6 5 4 3 2 1

Printed and bound in the United States of America

To Jim Ferman,
Chris Band, &
George Wilkinson

For trying to make a difference
in Wickenburg

Special thanks to...

Nancy Davis and Tracy O'Connell for their excellent proofreading and editing skills.

David Van Ness, for helping me fine-tune the book's layout and appearance.

Julie Bess, for delivering yet another great index.

Microsoft Corporation, for continuing to improve the world's best spreadsheet program.

To Mike, for the usual things.

contents

introduction   ix

what you'll create   x
how this book works   xii

the web site   xiv
the next step   xv

1. meet microsoft excel   1

learn the lingo   2
mouse around   3
start excel   4
look at excel   5
change the view   6
scroll a window   7

use the Ribbon   8
choose from a menu   10
have a dialog   12
exit excel   13
extra bits   14

2. create the workbook file   17

create the workbook   18
set display options   19

save the workbook   21
extra bits   22

3. build the budget worksheet   23

name the sheet   24
understand references   25
enter information   26
activate a cell   27
enter row headings   28
enter column headings   29

make a column wider   30
enter values   31
calculate a difference   33
calculate a percent diff   34
sum some values   35
calculate net income   37

contents

3. build the budget worksheet (cont'd)

copy formulas	38	change a value	43
copy and paste	39	extra bits	44
use the fill handle	40		

4. duplicate the worksheet   47

copy the sheet	48	delete a row	52
clear the values	49	enter new values	53
insert a row	51	extra bits	55

5. consolidate the results   57

prepare the sheet	58	calculate percent diff	64
consolidate	59	extra bits	65
check the consolidation	63		

6. format worksheets   67

set font formatting	68	add borders	77
format values	70	apply shading	79
format percentages	72	change text color	80
set column widths	73	format all worksheets	81
set alignment	75	extra bits	82
indent text	76		

contents

7. add a chart   85

hide a row	86	explode a pie	93
insert a chart	87	add data labels	95
create a chart sheet	88	format chart text	98
add a chart title	90	extra bits	99
move the legend	92		

8. share your work   101

switch to page layout	102	add a custom header	108
select the sheets	103	save settings	111
open page setup	104	preview the sheets	112
set page options	105	print your work	113
adjust margins	106	send via e-mail	114
add a standard footer	107	extra bits	116

index   119

introduction

This Visual QuickProject Guide offers a unique way to learn about new technologies. Instead of drowning you in theoretical possibilities and lengthy explanations, this Visual QuickProject Guide uses big, color illustrations coupled with clear, concise step-by-step instructions to show you how to complete a specific project in a matter of hours.

Our project in this book is to create an Excel workbook file that compares actual to budgeted income and expenses for three months, consolidates the results, and illustrates consolidated expenses as a pie chart. Although our example uses income and expense items for a fictional business, you can easily customize the worksheets for your own business or personal use. For example, you can create a worksheet that compares your personal budgeted and actual expenditures to see how well you're keeping to your budget. Or use the skills you'll learn throughout this book to keep track of your business's customer invoices and payments.

As you work through the project, you'll learn how to build worksheet files from the ground up, enter data and formulas, and copy formulas to save time. You'll see how powerful and flexible Excel is by working through examples that show off its most commonly used features. You'll try out Excel's consolidation feature and create and "explode" a colorful, three-dimensional chart. You'll also fine-tune the appearance of your worksheet files by applying all kinds of formatting. Along the way, you'll get plenty of ideas for how you can use Excel to crunch the numbers in your life.

what you'll create

Create a worksheet file that compares budgeted to actual income and expenses for a full month.

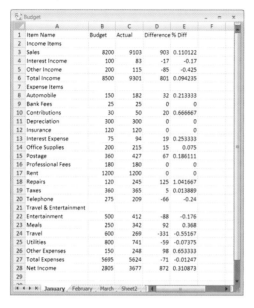

Duplicate the worksheet and modify the duplicates for two other months.

Create a consolidation that combines all information with live links to the source data.

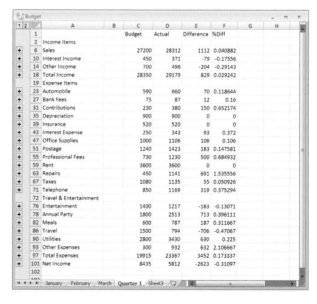

introduction

Format the worksheets so they look great when printed.

Print your worksheets, with custom headers and footers.

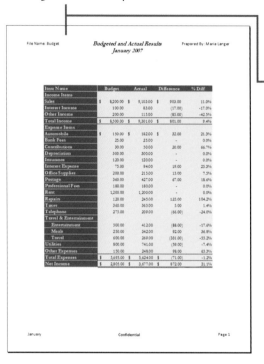

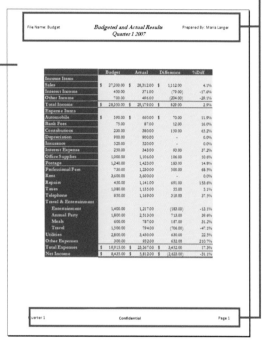

Create a colorful, "exploded" pie chart of consolidated expenses.

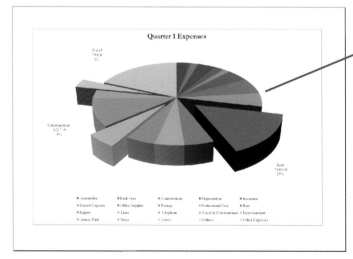

how this book works

The title of each section explains what is covered on that page.

Captions explain what you're seeing and why. They also point to relevant parts of Excel's interface.

---

sum some values

Although you can write a formula that adds multiple cell references, one cell at a time, it's much easier to use Excel's SUM function to add up the contents of a range of cells. Here are two ways to enter the SUM function in formulas to create subtotals for the values in column B.

An introductory sentence or paragraph summarizes what you'll do.

Use the AutoSum button:

Numbered steps explain actions to perform in a specific order.

1 Activate cell B6.

	A	B	C	
1	Item Name	Budget	Actual	Diff
2	Income Items			
3	Sales	8200	8103	
4	Interest Income	100	83	
5	Other Income	200	115	
6	Total Income			
7	Expense Items			
8	Automobile	150	182	
9	Book Fees	75	75	

2 Click the AutoSum button in the Editing group of the Ribbon's Home tab.

Excel writes a formula that uses the SUM function to add a range of cells. A colored box appears around the cells included in the formula.

	A	B	C	D
1	Item Name	Budget	Actual	Difference S
2	Income Items			
3	Sales	8200	8103	-97
4	Interest Income	100	83	
5	Other Income	200	115	
6	Total Income	=SUM(B3:B5)		
7	Expense Items	SUM(number1, [number2], ...)		
8	Automobile	150	182	

A function tooltip may appear as you enter the formula.

Important terms, names of interface elements, and text you should type exactly as shown appear in orange.

3 If the formula is correct (as shown here), press Enter.

If the formula is not correct, type in the correct range reference and press Enter.

The result of the formula appears in cell B6.

	A	B	C	
1	Item Name	Budget	Actual	Diff
2	Income Items			
3	Sales	8200	8103	
4	Interest Income	100	83	
5	Other Income	200	115	
6	Total Income	8500		
7	Expense Items			
8	Automobile	150	182	
9	Book Fees	75	75	

build the budget worksheet 35

The extra bits section at the end of each chapter contains additional tips and tricks that you might like to know—but that aren't absolutely necessary.

enter values

The heading for each group of tips matches the section title.

extra bits

name the sheet p. 24
- As you'll see in Chapter 8, you can instruct Excel to automatically display a sheet name in a printed report's header or footer. That's a good reason to give a sheet an appropriate name.

activate a cell p. 27
- When you use the point-and-click method for activating a cell, you must click. If you don't click, the cell pointer won't move and the cell you're pointing to won't be activated.

enter row headings p. 28
- When you enter text in a cell, Excel's AutoComplete feature may suggest entries based on previous entries in the column.

12	Insurance
13	Interest Expense
14	Office Supplies
15	Postage
16	Postage
17	

To accept an entry, press Enter when it appears. Otherwise, just keep typing what you want to enter. The AutoComplete suggestion will eventually go away.

make a column wider p. 30
- You can't change the width of a single cell. You must change the width of the entire column the cell is in.

enter values pp. 31–32
- You can enter any values you like in this step. But if you enter the same values I do, you can later compare the results of your formulas to mine to make sure the formulas you enter in the next step are correct.
- Do not include currency symbols or commas when entering values. Doing so will apply number formatting. I explain how to format cell contents, including values, in Chapter 6.
- If you use the arrow keys to move from one cell to the next, the selection area disappears. Although you can enter values without a selection area, using a selection area makes it easier to move from one cell to another.
- If, after entering values, you discover that one of the values is incorrect, activate the cell with the incorrect value, enter the correct value, and press Enter to save it.

The page number(s) next to the heading makes it easy to refer back to the main content.

build the budget worksheet

the web site

Find this book's companion Web site at:
http://www.marialanger.com/excelquickproject/.

Read timely articles about getting the most out of Excel.

Access a list of frequently asked questions and answers.

Share your comments and tips with other site visitors.

Download sample files used in the book.

Access excerpts from the book.

Content is updated regularly with news, tips, and more.

the next step

While this Visual QuickProject Guide will walk you through all of the steps required to create and format worksheets and charts, there's more to learn about Excel. After you complete this project, consider picking up my more advanced Excel book— Microsoft Office Excel 2007 for Windows: Visual QuickStart Guide—as a handy, in-depth reference.

VISUAL QUICKSTART GUIDE

MICROSOFT OFFICE
EXCEL 2007

Learn Excel the Quick and Easy Way!

OR WINDOWS   **MARIA LANGER**

This book includes more advanced information about using Excel to create worksheets, lists, and charts. It tells you about all the options you see in Excel tabs, groups, and dialogs, explains how to customize Excel so it works the way you need it to, and provides detailed, step-by-step instructions for using basic, intermediate, and advanced Excel features.

1. meet microsoft excel

Microsoft Excel is a full-featured spreadsheet program that you can use to build worksheets and charts like the ones you'll create with this book.

As you work with Excel, you'll see that it has some of the same interface elements you're familiar with from using your other Windows programs: windows, menus, dialogs, and buttons. It also has a bunch of new interface elements Microsoft developed for Microsoft Office 2007 programs: the Ribbon with its tabs, groups, and commands.

In this chapter, I introduce you to Excel's interface elements and tell you about the techniques you'll need to know to use Excel. If this project is your first hands-on experience with Excel or your computer, be sure to read through this chapter!

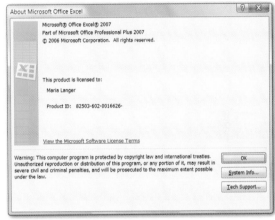

This book covers Microsoft Excel 2007 for Windows. Although most screenshots show Excel running on Microsoft's Windows Vista operating system, Excel 2007 also runs on Windows XP.

learn the lingo

Before you start working with Excel, let me review a few of the terms I'll use throughout this book. If you've been working with your computer for a while, this may seem a bit basic, but I do want to make sure we're on the same page (so to speak) as we work through this project.

An icon is a graphical representation of a file.

EXCEL

Here's what the Excel program icon looks like.

Expenses

And here's what an Excel document icon looks like.

Windows Explorer is the Windows program that you use to work with files.

If you need to learn more about using Windows, be sure to check out Microsoft Windows Vista: Visual QuickStart Guide or Windows XP: Visual QuickStart Guide, Second Edition by Chris Fehily.

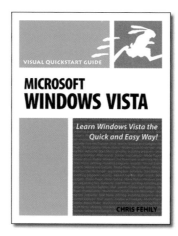

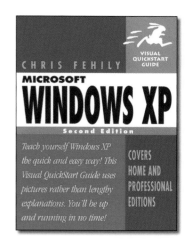

meet microsoft excel

mouse around

The white arrow that appears on your screen is the mouse pointer. Move your mouse and the mouse pointer moves.

Point means to position the tip of the mouse pointer on something. For example, you can point to a Ribbon tab...  ...or point to a command or button.

The mouse pointer can also change its appearance when you point to other things. For example, if you point to a cell in an Excel worksheet window, it changes into a cross pointer...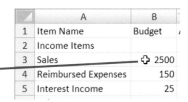

...and if you point to a column heading in an Excel worksheet window, it changes to an arrow pointing down.

You use the button(s) on your mouse to click, double-click, and drag.

Click means to press and release the left mouse button.

Right-click means to press and release the right mouse button.

Double-click means to click twice fast—without moving the mouse between clicks.

Drag means to point to something, hold the mouse button down, and move the mouse. You use this technique to move icons, select text, and perform other tasks.

A typical Windows mouse has two buttons.

start excel

In Windows, you start a program to use it.

1 Click Start to display the Start menu.

2 Click All Programs.

3 Click Microsoft Office.

4 Click Microsoft Office Excel 2007.

In Windows Vista:

In Windows XP:

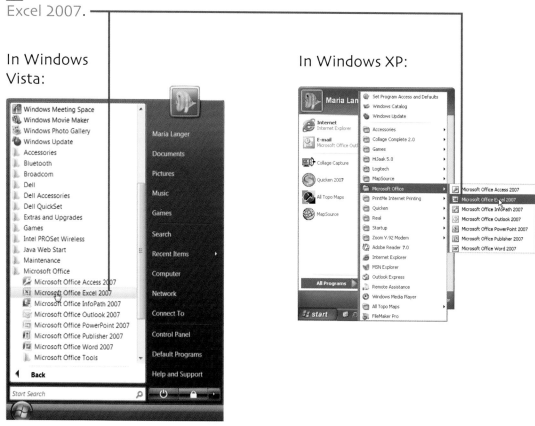

Excel starts and an untitled workbook window appears, as shown on page 5.

meet microsoft excel

look at excel

Here are some of the important interface elements in Excel 2007.

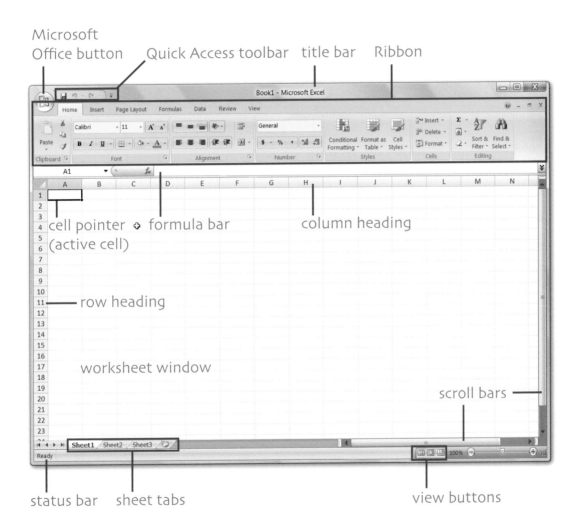

Microsoft Office button · Quick Access toolbar · title bar · Ribbon

cell pointer ✛ · formula bar · column heading

(active cell)

row heading

worksheet window

scroll bars

status bar · sheet tabs · view buttons

change the view

Excel 2007 has three views: Normal, Page Layout View, and Page Break Preview.

To change a window's view:

1 Click the View tab on the Ribbon.

2 In the Workbook Views group, click the command button for the view you want.

You can also change a window's view by clicking one of the View buttons at the bottom-right of the window. As shown here, you can point to a button to determine which view it's for.

Throughout most of this book, we'll stick to Normal view, which is illustrated on page 5.

meet microsoft excel

scroll a window

Scroll bars on a window make it possible to shift window contents up or down (or sideways) to see hidden contents.

A vertical scroll bar:

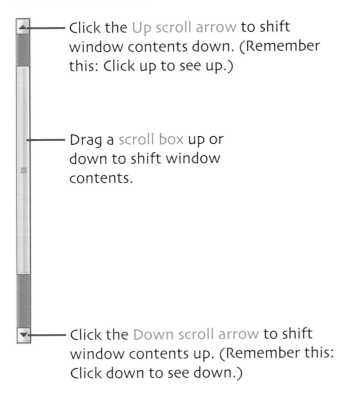

Click the Up scroll arrow to shift window contents down. (Remember this: Click up to see up.)

Drag a scroll box up or down to shift window contents.

Click the Down scroll arrow to shift window contents up. (Remember this: Click down to see down.)

A horizontal scroll bar:

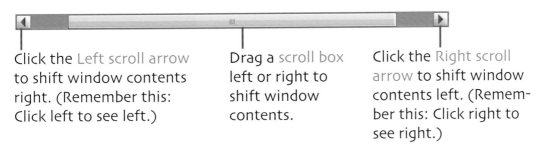

Click the Left scroll arrow to shift window contents right. (Remember this: Click left to see left.)

Drag a scroll box left or right to shift window contents.

Click the Right scroll arrow to shift window contents left. (Remember this: Click right to see right.)

use the Ribbon

The Ribbon gives you access to all of Excel's commands.

The Ribbon is organized into tabs, each of which have multiple groups of commands. As shown here, commands can be buttons, menus, check boxes or text boxes.

tab   group   command

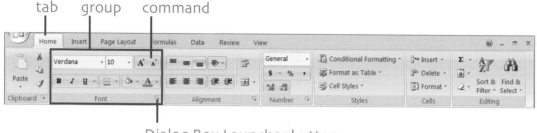

Dialog Box Launcher button

1 Click the tab for the task you want to complete.

2 Access the command you want by clicking its button,...

Pointing to a command displays a ScreenTip box with information about the command.

...choosing an option from its menu,...

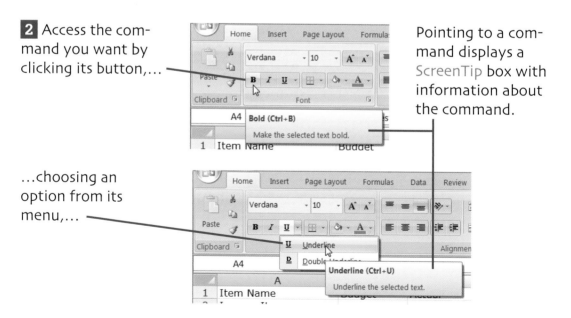

meet microsoft excel

...turning on its check box,...

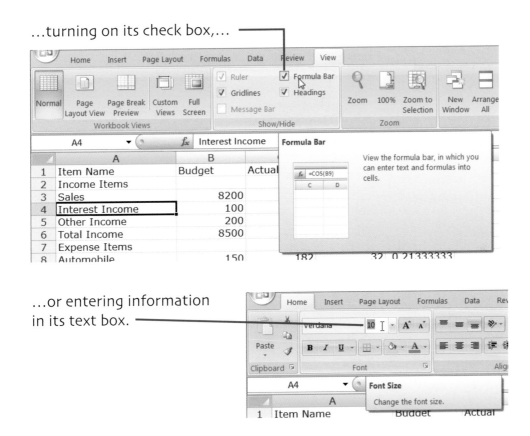

...or entering information in its text box.

Excel displays additional Ribbon tabs called tools when certain types of objects are selected. For example, if a chart is selected, the Chart Tools tabs appear, as shown here:

choose from a menu

Excel has several different types of menus.

Ribbon commands that include an arrow or triangle display a menu when you click them.

To choose a menu command, click to display the menu, then click the command you want.

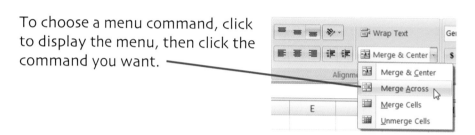

The Microsoft Office menu is a list of file-related commands accessible from a big round button at the top-left of the Excel application window.

To display the Microsoft Office menu, click its button.

To choose a menu command, click it.

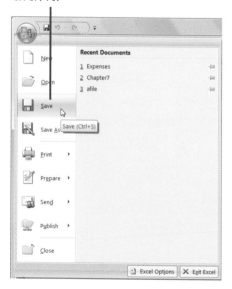

meet microsoft excel

A submenu is a menu that pops out of another menu when you select it.

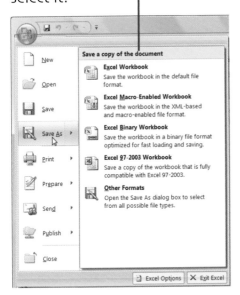

To choose a submenu command, display the submenu and click the command. ￢

A contextual menu appears when you right-click something.

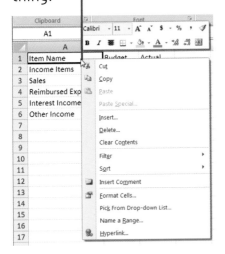

To choose a contextual menu command, display the menu and click the command.

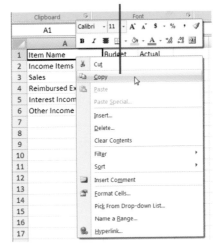

meet microsoft excel

have a dialog

A dialog (or dialog box) is a window that appears onscreen when your computer needs to communicate with you.

When a dialog offers options for you to complete a task, it can display the options in a number of ways.

Tabs let you switch from one group of settings to another.

Scrolling lists offer multiple options in a list.

Check boxes are for turning an option on or off. Click a check box to toggle its setting.

Text boxes are fields you can fill in by typing.

Drop-down lists offer multiple options when you click them.

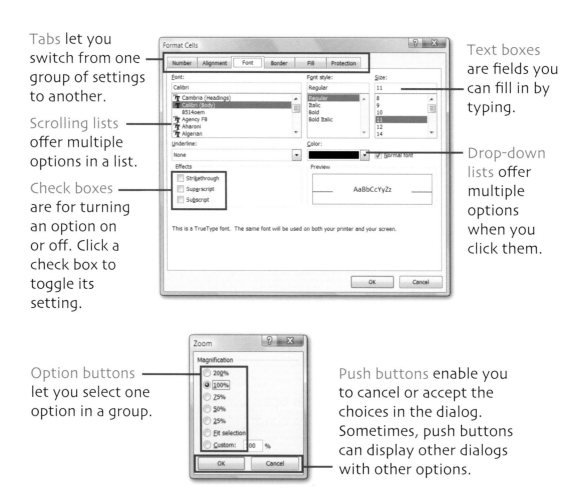

Option buttons let you select one option in a group.

Push buttons enable you to cancel or accept the choices in the dialog. Sometimes, push buttons can display other dialogs with other options.

meet microsoft excel

exit excel

When you're finished using Excel, you should exit it.

Choose Exit Excel
from the Microsoft
Office menu.

If a document with unsaved changes is open,
Excel displays a dialog that gives you a chance
to save the document. (I tell you how to save
documents in Chapter 2.)

extra bits

mouse around p. 3

- It's possible to get a three-button mouse for your PC. Frankly, I think two buttons are confusing enough, so I'll assume that's all your mouse has.

- You can also get a mouse with a roller—in fact, it's pretty common for Windows. You can use the roller to scroll an active window. Since this feature doesn't work consistently and not everyone has a roller, I don't discuss it in this book.

start excel p. 4

- These instructions assume you have installed the entire Microsoft Office suite of products, including Excel, Word, PowerPoint, and Outlook. If you have installed just Excel on your computer, consult the documentation that came with it for instructions on how to start it.

- Your Start menu probably won't look exactly like mine. But if you follow the instructions, you should be able to find and start Excel using your Start menu.

- There are lots of ways to start Excel in Windows. If you have a method you prefer, go for it!

look at excel p. 5

- If you've used previous versions of Excel, you probably noticed that Excel 2007 looks very different. Microsoft's new Ribbon-based interface makes considerable changes in the way Excel looks and works. Commands are now better organized and more easily accessible than in any previous version of Excel.

- If the formula bar does not appear, click the View tab on the Ribbon and toggle the Formula Bar option in the Show/Hide group. I explain how to use the Ribbon on page 8.

use the Ribbon pp. 8–9

- The number of commands that appear in a group on a Ribbon's tab can vary depending on the size and resolution of your computer screen. The wider your screen or the higher the resolution, the more commands appear. For example, compare the Home tab shown on page 8 with the one on page 5, which is much wider.

- To display the most commands on the Ribbon, it's a good idea to set your screen resolution at a comfortably high setting and maximize the Excel application window. You can use the Windows Control Panel to set screen resolution. To maximize the Excel application window, click the Maximize button in the upper-right corner, beside the Close button.

- You can customize the format of the ScreenTips that appear when you point to a command. Choose Microsoft Office Button > Excel Options. Click Popular in the Excel Options window that appears. Then choose an option from the ScreenTip style drop-down list. Click OK to save your changes.

choose from a menu pp. 10–11

- The Microsoft Office menu replaces the File menu that appeared in previous versions of Excel and other Microsoft Office programs.

- Contextual menus are sometimes known as shortcut menus.

have a dialog p. 12

- Clicking the Dialog Box Launcher button in the bottom-right corner of a Ribbon group displays a dialog full of related options.

- You can select any number of check boxes in a group, but you can select only one option button in a group.

exit excel p. 13

- A quick way to exit Excel is to double-click the Microsoft Office button.

extra bits (cont'd)

shortcut keys

- If a shortcut key combination appears in a ScreenTip box when you point to a command, you can use that key combination to invoke the command without using your mouse. For example, as shown on page 8, the ScreenTip for the Bold command indicates that pressing Ctrl + B invokes that command. (Hold down Ctrl and press B.) I tell you about shortcut keys for commands used in this project in the extra bits section at the end of each chapter.

meet microsoft excel

2. create the workbook file

Excel documents are called workbook files. A workbook can include multiple sheets of information.

Excel supports two kinds of sheets for working with data:

• Worksheets, which are also known as spreadsheets, are for recording text and numerical information and performing calculations. Our project will use worksheets for the monthly budget information and the consolidation.

• Chart sheets are for displaying worksheet information as graphs or charts. Excel supports many types of charts, including the pie chart that's part of our project.

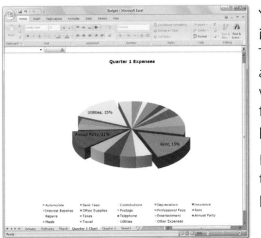

You can think of Excel sheets as pages in an Excel book—that's what I do. Then, when you create a workbook for a project—like our monthly budget with consolidation and chart—you can fill it with the sheets that apply to that project to keep everything together.

In this chapter, we'll create and save the workbook file we'll use to build our project.

create the workbook

Excel offers a number of ways to create a blank workbook file. One way is with the New command.

1 Click the Microsoft Office button.

2 Click the New command.

The New Workbook dialog appears.

3 Click Blank and recent in the Templates list.

4 Click Blank Workbook.

5 Click Create.

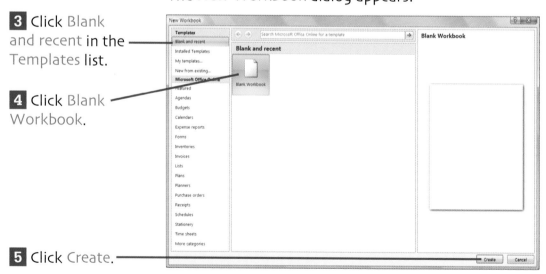

A new workbook document appears. It displays a worksheet window, like the one on page 5.

create the workbook file

set display options

You can set display options to determine which screen elements appear while you're working with Excel. It's a good idea to display the tools you'll need to complete this project before you start creating worksheets.

1 Click the Microsoft Office button.

2 Click the Excel Options button. ——

3 In the Excel Options dialog that appears, click Advanced to display Advanced options for working with Excel.

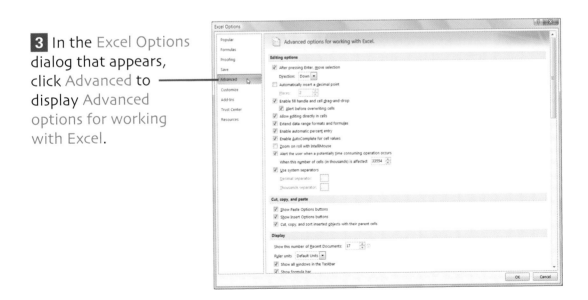

set display options (cont'd)

4 Under Display, make sure the Show formula bar check box is turned on.

Scroll down to see the options you need to set.

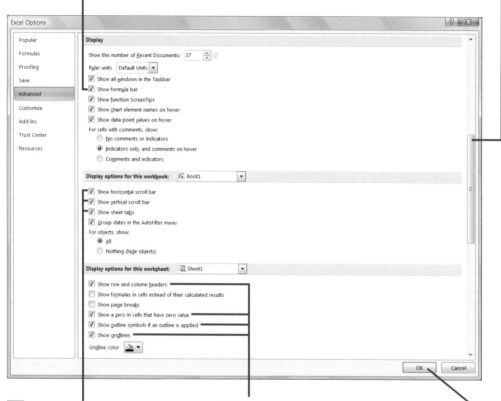

5 Under Display options for this workbook, make sure the following check boxes are turned on:

- Show horizontal scroll bar
- Show vertical scroll bar
- Show sheet tabs

6 Under Display options for this worksheet, make sure the following check boxes are turned on:

- Show row and column headers
- Show a zero in cells that have zero value
- Show outline symbols if an outline is applied
- Show gridlines

7 Click OK.

create the workbook file

save the workbook

You can save a workbook file to keep a record of it on disk or to open and work with it at a later date. For this project, we'll save the workbook in the Documents folder.

1 Choose Save from the Microsoft Office menu.

The Save As dialog appears. You use this dialog to set options for saving the file.

2 Click the Browse Folders button to expand the dialog.

3 Click the Documents folder in the Folders list to display a list of files and folders in your Documents folder.

4 Type Budget in the File name box.

5 Choose Excel Workbook from the Save as type drop-down list.

6 Click Save.

The document is saved in your Documents folder. Its name appears in the title bar.

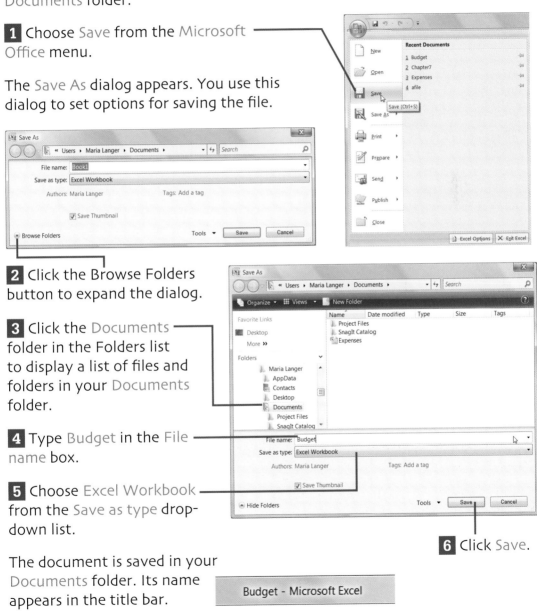

extra bits

create the workbook p. 18

- A new workbook is automatically created when you launch the Excel program.

save the workbook p. 21

- It's a good idea to save your workbook file occasionally as you build it. Just choose Save from the Microsoft Office menu, click the Save button on the Quick Access toolbar (shown here), or hold down Ctrl while pressing S. Excel saves the current version of the file without displaying a dialog.

- To save a file with a different name or in a different disk location, choose Save As from the Microsoft Office menu. Then set options in the Save As dialog that appears to save a copy of the file. Remember that the original version of the file remains on disk but is not updated with any changes that you made since you saved it.

- If you're running Excel 2007 on Windows XP instead of Windows Vista, the Save As dialog will look different. Save the file into your My Documents folder, which you can quickly open by clicking its icon in the dialog's sidebar.

shortcut keys for this chapter

New	Ctrl + N
Save	Ctrl-S
Save As	F12

3. build the budget worksheet

The primary element of our project is the monthly budget worksheet. This worksheet lists all of the income and expense categories with columns for budgeted amounts, actual amounts, dollar difference, and percent difference. It also includes subtotals and totals.

As you can see, an Excel worksheet window closely resembles an accountant's paper worksheet. It includes columns and rows that intersect at cells. To build our budget worksheet, we'll enter information into cells.

In this chapter, we'll create the budget worksheet as shown here. (We'll apply formatting to the worksheet so it looks more presentable later in this project.)

	A	B	C	D	E
1	Item Name	Budget	Actual	Difference	% Diff
2	Income Items				
3	Sales	8200	9103	903	0.110122
4	Interest Income	100	83	-17	-0.17
5	Other Income	200	115	-85	-0.425
6	Total Income	8500	9301	801	0.094235
7	Expense Items				
8	Automobile	150	182	32	0.213333
9	Bank Fees	25	25	0	0
10	Contributions	30	50	20	0.666667
11	Depreciation	300	300	0	0
12	Insurance	120	120	0	0
13	Interest Expense	75	94	19	0.253333
14	Office Supplies	200	215	15	0.075
15	Postage	360	427	67	0.186111
16	Professional Fees	180	180	0	0
17	Rent	1200	1200	0	0
18	Repairs	120	245	125	1.041667
19	Taxes	360	365	5	0.013889
20	Telephone	275	209	-66	-0.24
21	Travel & Entertainment				
22	Entertainment	500	412	-88	-0.176
23	Meals	250	342	92	0.368
24	Travel	600	269	-331	-0.55167
25	Utilities	800	741	-59	-0.07375
26	Other Expenses	150	248	98	0.653333
27	Total Expenses	5695	5624	-71	-0.01247
28	Net Income	2805	3677	872	0.310873
29					

name the sheet

The sheet tabs at the bottom of the worksheet window enable you to iden-tify the active sheet. Each new workbook file includes three worksheets named Sheet1, Sheet2, and Sheet3. You can change the name of a sheet to make it more descriptive.

It's easy to identify the active sheet. Its sheet tab is white and the sheet name appears in bold text. And, if you have sharp eyes, you may notice that the active sheet's tab seems to appear on top of the other tabs.

1 Double-click the Sheet1 sheet tab. The name of the tab becomes selected.

2 Type January. The text you type overwrites the selected sheet name.

3 Press Enter. The new name is saved.

build the budget worksheet

understand references

The concept of references or addressing is important when working with spreadsheets. A reference or address identifies the part of the worksheet that you are working with.

Columns are referred to with letters.

For example, this is column H.

Rows are referred to with numbers.

For example, this is row 9.

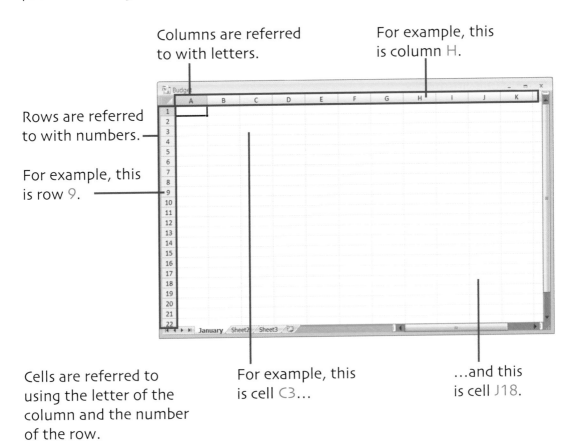

Cells are referred to using the letter of the column and the number of the row.

For example, this is cell C3...

...and this is cell J18.

enter information

To build the budget worksheet, you'll enter three kinds of information into Excel worksheet cells:

- Labels (shown here in orange) are text entries that are used to identify information in the worksheet. For example, the word Budget is a label that will appear at the top of the column containing budget information.

- Values (shown here in green) are numbers, dates, or times. Values differ from labels in that you can perform mathematical calculations on them. In our budget worksheet, you'll enter numbers as values for budget and actual information.

- Formulas (shown here in yellow) are calculations written in a special notation that Excel can understand. When you enter a formula in a cell, Excel

	A	B	C	D	E
1	Item Name	Budget	Actual	Difference	% Diff
2	Income Items				
3	Sales	8200	9103	903	0.110121951
4	Interest Income	100	83	-17	-0.17
5	Other Income	200	115	-85	-0.425
6	Total Income	8500	9301	801	0.094235294
7	Expense Items				
8	Automobile	150	182	32	0.213333333
9	Bank Fees	25	25	0	0
10	Contributions	30	50	20	0.666666667
11	Depreciation	300	300	0	0
12	Insurance	120	120	0	0
13	Interest Expense	75	94	19	0.253333333
14	Office Supplies	200	215	15	0.075
15	Postage	360	427	67	0.186111111
16	Professional Fees	180	180	0	0
17	Rent	1200	1200	0	0
18	Repairs	120	245	125	1.041666667
19	Taxes	360	365	5	0.013888889
20	Telephone	275	209	-66	-0.24
21	Travel & Entertainment				
22	Entertainment	500	412	-88	-0.176
23	Meals	250	342	92	0.368
24	Travel	600	269	-331	-0.551666667
25	Utilities	800	741	-59	-0.07375
26	Other Expenses	150	248	98	0.653333333
27	Total Expenses	5695	5624	-71	-0.012467076
28	Net Income	2805	3677	872	0.31087344

displays the result of the formula, not the formula itself. Formulas are a powerful feature of spreadsheet programs because they can perform all kinds of simple and complex calculations for you. In our budget worksheet, we'll use formulas to calculate the difference between budget and actual information in dollars and percents and to calculate column subtotals and totals.

build the budget worksheet

activate a cell

To enter information into a cell, you must activate it. That means moving the cell pointer to the cell in which you want to enter a label, value, or formula.

There are lots of ways to move the cell pointer, but rather than bombard you with a lot of unnecessary options, I'll tell you the two ways I use most.

Point and click:

1 Move the mouse pointer, which looks like a cross, over the cell you want to activate.

2 Press the mouse button once. The cell pointer moves to the cell you pointed to.

Use the arrow keys:

On the keyboard, press the arrow key corresponding to the direction you want the cell pointer to move.

For example, in this illustration, if I wanted to move the cell pointer from cell C8 to cell D6…

…I'd press the right arrow key once…   …and the up arrow key twice.

enter row headings

The row headings in our budget worksheet will identify the categories of income and expenses and label the subtotals and net income.

1 Activate cell A1 (the first cell in the worksheet).

2 Type Item Name.

3 Press Enter. The cell pointer moves down one cell.

4 Repeat steps 2 and 3 for the following labels:

Income Items	Professional Fees
Sales	Rent
Interest Income	Repairs
Other Income	Taxes
Total Income	Telephone
Expense Items	Travel & Entertainment
Automobile	Entertainment
Bank Fees	Meals
Contributions	Travel
Depreciation	Utilities
Insurance	Other Expenses
Interest Expense	Total Expenses
Office Supplies	Net Income
Postage	

When you're finished, the worksheet should look like this:

enter column headings

Our budget worksheet includes several columns of data and calculations. We'll use column headings to identify them.

1 Activate cell B1 (the one to the right of where you entered Item Name).

	A	B	C	D	E	F
1	Item Name					
2	Income Items					
3	Sales					

2 Type Budget.

	A	B	C	D	E	F
1	Item Name	Budget				
2	Income Items					
3	Sales					

3 Press Tab. The cell pointer moves one cell to the right.

	A	B	C	D	E	F
1	Item Name	Budget				
2	Income Items					
3	Sales					

4 Repeat steps 2 and 3 for the following labels:

Actual
Difference
% Diff

When you're finished, the worksheet should look like this:

	A	B	C	D	E	F
1	Item Name	Budget	Actual	Difference	% Diff	
2	Income Items					
3	Sales					

make a column wider

If the text in a cell has too many characters to fit in that cell, part of the cell's contents may appear truncated when you enter information in the cell to its right.

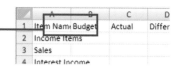

All the information you entered is still there; it's just hidden because the column it's in is too narrow. You can use Excel's AutoWidth feature to quickly make a column wider.

1 Position the mouse pointer on the right border of column A. The mouse pointer turns into a bar with two arrows coming out of it.

2 Double-click. The column automatically widens to accommodate the widest text in the column.

Have you been saving your work?

Now is a good time to click the Save button on the Quick Access toolbar to save your work up to this point.

build the budget worksheet

enter values

The whole purpose of the worksheet is to compare budgeted to actual amounts. It's time to enter those amounts. Since we need to enter values in two columns, we'll use an entry selection area.

1 Position the mouse pointer over cell B3.

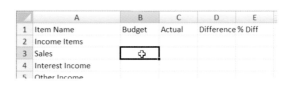

2 Press the mouse button down and drag down and to the right to cell C26. All cells between B3 and C26 are enclosed in a selection box, but cell B3 remains the active cell.

3 Type 8200.
It appears in cell B3.

4 Press Enter. Cell B4 becomes the active cell.

enter values (cont'd)

5 Repeat steps 3 and 4 for the remaining values in column B as shown here. When a cell that should remain blank becomes active, just press Enter again to make the next cell active. After entering the last value in the column, when you press Enter, cell C3 becomes active.

	A	B	C	
1	Item Name	Budget	Actual	Diffe
2	Income Items			
3	Sales	8200		
4	Interest Income	100		
5	Other Income	200		
6	Total Income			
7	Expense Items			
8	Automobile	150		
9	Bank Fees	25		
10	Contributions	30		
11	Depreciation	300		
12	Insurance	120		
13	Interest Expense	75		
14	Office Supplies	200		
15	Postage	360		
16	Professional Fees	180		
17	Rent	1200		
18	Repairs	120		
19	Taxes	360		
20	Telephone	275		
21	Travel & Entertainment			
22	Entertainment	500		
23	Meals	250		
24	Travel	600		
25	Utilities	800		
26	Other Expenses	150		
27	Total Expenses			
28	Net Income			

6 Repeat steps 3 and 4 for the values in column C as shown here. When a cell that should remain blank becomes active, just press Enter again to make the next cell active. After entering the last value in the column, when you press Enter, cell B3 becomes active again.

	A	B	C	
1	Item Name	Budget	Actual	Diffe
2	Income Items			
3	Sales	8200	8103	
4	Interest Income	100	83	
5	Other Income	200	115	
6	Total Income			
7	Expense Items			
8	Automobile	150	182	
9	Bank Fees	25	25	
10	Contributions	30	50	
11	Depreciation	300	300	
12	Insurance	120	120	
13	Interest Expense	75	94	
14	Office Supplies	200	215	
15	Postage	360	427	
16	Professional Fees	180	180	
17	Rent	1200	1200	
18	Repairs	120	245	
19	Taxes	360	365	
20	Telephone	275	209	
21	Travel & Entertainment			
22	Entertainment	500	412	
23	Meals	250	342	
24	Travel	600	269	
25	Utilities	800	741	
26	Other Expenses	150	248	
27	Total Expenses			
28	Net Income			

7 Click anywhere in the worksheet window to deselect the selected cells.

build the budget worksheet

calculate a difference

Column D, which will display the difference between budgeted and actual amounts, will contain simple formulas that subtract one cell's contents from another's using cell references. In this step, we'll write the first formula. Later, we'll copy the formula to other cells in the column.

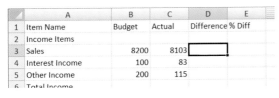

1 Activate cell D3.

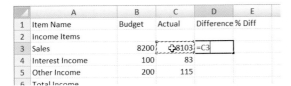

2 Type =.

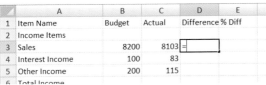

3 Click in cell C3.

Its cell reference appears in cell D3.

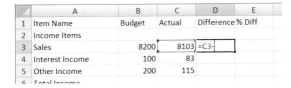

4 Type −.

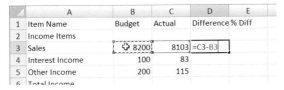

5 Click in cell B3.

Its cell reference is appended to the formula in cell D3.

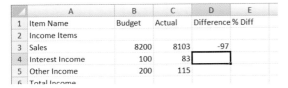

6 Press Enter.

The result of the formula you entered appears in cell D3.

calculate a percent diff

Column E calculates the percent difference between the budgeted and actual amounts. The percentage is based on the budgeted amount. We'll write the first formula now and copy it to other cells in column E later.

1 Activate cell E3.

2 Type =.

3 Click in cell D3.

Its cell reference appears in cell E3.

4 Type /.

5 Click in cell B3.

Its cell reference is appended to the formula in cell E3.

6 Press Enter.

The result of the formula you entered appears in cell E3.

build the budget worksheet

sum some values

Although you can write a formula that adds multiple cell references, one cell at a time, it's much easier to use Excel's SUM function to add up the contents of a range of cells. Here are two ways to enter the SUM function in formulas to create subtotals for the values in column B.

Use the AutoSum button:

1 Activate cell B6.

	A	B	C	
1	Item Name	Budget	Actual	Diff
2	Income Items			
3	Sales	8200	8103	
4	Interest Income	100	83	
5	Other Income	200	115	
6	Total Income			
7	Expense Items			
8	Automobile	150	182	
9	Bank Fees	25	25	

2 Click the AutoSum button in the Editing group of the Ribbon's Home tab.

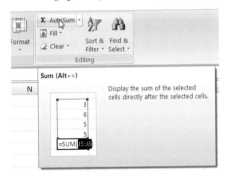

Excel writes a formula that uses the SUM function to add a range of cells. A colored box appears around the cells included in the formula.

	A	B	C	D
1	Item Name	Budget	Actual	Difference %
2	Income Items			
3	Sales	8200	8103	-97
4	Interest Income	100	83	
5	Other Income	200	115	
6	Total Income	=SUM(B3:B5)		
7	Expense Items	SUM(**number1**, [number2], ...)		
8	Automobile	150	182	
9	Bank Fees	25	25	

A function tooltip may appear as you enter the formula.

3 If the formula is correct (as shown here), press Enter.

If the formula is not correct, type in the correct range reference and press Enter.

The result of the formula appears in cell B6.

	A	B	C	
1	Item Name	Budget	Actual	Diff
2	Income Items			
3	Sales	8200	8103	
4	Interest Income	100	83	
5	Other Income	200	115	
6	Total Income	8500		
7	Expense Items			
8	Automobile	150	182	
9	Bank Fees	25	25	

build the budget worksheet 35

sum some values (cont'd)

Type and drag:

1 Activate cell B27.

	A	B	C	
1	Item Name	Budget	Actual	
2	Income Items			
3	Sales	8200	8103	
4	Interest Income	100	83	
5	Other Income	200	115	
6	Total Income	8500		
7	Expense Items			
8	Automobile	150	182	
9	Bank Fees	25	25	
10	Contributions	30	50	
11	Depreciation	300	300	
12	Insurance	120	120	
13	Interest Expense	75	94	
14	Office Supplies	200	215	
15	Postage	360	427	
16	Professional Fees	180	180	
17	Rent	1200	1200	
18	Repairs	120	245	
19	Taxes	360	365	
20	Telephone	275	209	
21	Travel & Entertainment			
22	Entertainment	500	412	
23	Meals	250	342	
24	Travel	600	269	
25	Utilities	800	741	
26	Other Expenses	150	248	
27	Total Expenses			
28	Net Income			

2 Type =SUM(.

25	Utilities	800	741
26	Other Expenses	150	248
27	Total Expenses	=sum(	
28	Net Income	SUM(**number1**, [number2], ...)	

A function tooltip may appear as you enter the formula.

3 Position the mouse pointer on cell B8.

	A	B	
1	Item Name	Budget	Act
2	Income Items		
3	Sales	8200	
4	Interest Income	100	
5	Other Income	200	
6	Total Income	8500	
7	Expense Items		
8	Automobile	⇩ 150	
9	Bank Fees	25	
10	Contributions	30	

4 Press the mouse button and drag down to cell B26. All cells you dragged over are selected and referenced in the formula in cell B27.

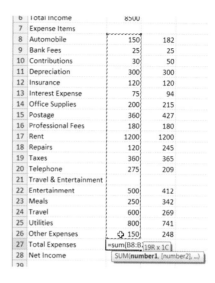

6	Total Income	8500	
7	Expense Items		
8	Automobile	150	182
9	Bank Fees	25	25
10	Contributions	30	50
11	Depreciation	300	300
12	Insurance	120	120
13	Interest Expense	75	94
14	Office Supplies	200	215
15	Postage	360	427
16	Professional Fees	180	180
17	Rent	1200	1200
18	Repairs	120	245
19	Taxes	360	365
20	Telephone	275	209
21	Travel & Entertainment		
22	Entertainment	500	412
23	Meals	250	342
24	Travel	600	269
25	Utilities	800	741
26	Other Expenses	⇩ 150	248
27	Total Expenses	=sum(B8:B 19R x 1C	
28	Net Income	SUM(**number1**, [number2], ...)	

5 Type).

6	Total Income	8500	
7	Expense Items		
8	Automobile	150	182
9	Bank Fees	25	25
10	Contributions	30	50
11	Depreciation	300	300
12	Insurance	120	120
13	Interest Expense	75	94
14	Office Supplies	200	215
15	Postage	360	427
16	Professional Fees	180	180
17	Rent	1200	1200
18	Repairs	120	245
19	Taxes	360	365
20	Telephone	275	209
21	Travel & Entertainment		
22	Entertainment	500	412
23	Meals	250	342
24	Travel	600	269
25	Utilities	800	741
26	Other Expenses	150	248
27	Total Expenses	=sum(B8:B26)	
28	Net Income		

6 Press Enter. The formula result appears in cell B27.

24	Travel	600	209
25	Utilities	800	741
26	Other Expenses	150	248
27	Total Expenses	5695	
28	Net Income		

build the budget worksheet

calculate net income

The final row of the worksheet contains cells to calculate the net income (total income minus total expenses). Here's how to enter that final formula:

1 Activate cell B28.

25	Utilities	800
26	Other Expenses	150
27	Total Expenses	5695
28	Net Income	
29		

2 Type =.

25	Utilities	800
26	Other Expenses	150
27	Total Expenses	5695
28	Net Income	=
29		

3 Click cell B6. Its reference appears in the formula in cell B28.

	A	B
1	Item Name	Budget
2	Income Items	
3	Sales	8200
4	Interest Income	100
5	Other Income	200
6	Total Income	8500
7	Expense Items	
8	Automobile	150
9	Bank Fees	25
10	Contributions	30
11	Depreciation	300
12	Insurance	120
13	Interest Expense	75
14	Office Supplies	200
15	Postage	360
16	Professional Fees	180
17	Rent	1200
18	Repairs	120
19	Taxes	360
20	Telephone	275
21	Travel & Entertainment	
22	Entertainment	500
23	Meals	250
24	Travel	600
25	Utilities	800
26	Other Expenses	150
27	Total Expenses	5695
28	Net Income	=B6
29		

4 Type −.

	A	B
1	Item Name	Budget
2	Income Items	
3	Sales	8200
4	Interest Income	100
5	Other Income	200
6	Total Income	8500
7	Expense Items	
8	Automobile	150
9	Bank Fees	25
10	Contributions	30
11	Depreciation	300
12	Insurance	120
13	Interest Expense	75
14	Office Supplies	200
15	Postage	360
16	Professional Fees	180
17	Rent	1200
18	Repairs	120
19	Taxes	360
20	Telephone	275
21	Travel & Entertainment	
22	Entertainment	500
23	Meals	250
24	Travel	600
25	Utilities	800
26	Other Expenses	150
27	Total Expenses	5695
28	Net Income	=B6-
29		

5 Click cell B27. Its reference appears in the formula in cell B28.

	A	B
1	Item Name	Budget
2	Income Items	
3	Sales	8200
4	Interest Income	100
5	Other Income	200
6	Total Income	8500
7	Expense Items	
8	Automobile	150
9	Bank Fees	25
10	Contributions	30
11	Depreciation	300
12	Insurance	120
13	Interest Expense	75
14	Office Supplies	200
15	Postage	360
16	Professional Fees	180
17	Rent	1200
18	Repairs	120
19	Taxes	360
20	Telephone	275
21	Travel & Entertainment	
22	Entertainment	500
23	Meals	250
24	Travel	600
25	Utilities	800
26	Other Expenses	150
27	Total Expenses	5695
28	Net Income	=B6-B27
29		

6 Press Enter. The result of the formula appears in cell B28.

26	Other Expenses	150
27	Total Expenses	5695
28	Net Income	2805
29		
30		

Have you been saving your work?

Now is a good time to click the Save button on the Quick Access toolbar to save your work up to this point.

Save (Ctrl+S)

build the budget worksheet

copy formulas

Excel lets you copy a formula in one cell to another cell that needs a similar formula. This can save a lot of time when building a worksheet with multiple columns or rows that need similar formulas.

For example, you can copy the formula in cell B6 (total income for budgeted amounts) to cell C6 (total income for actual amounts).

	A	B	C
1	Item Name	Budget	Actual
2	Income Items		
3	Sales	8200	8103
4	Interest Income	100	83
5	Other Income	200	115
6	Total Income	8500	8301

$= SUM(B3:B5)$
$= SUM(C3:C5)$

	A	B	C	D
1	Item Name	Budget	Actual	Difference
2	Income Items			
3	Sales	8200	8103	-97
4	Interest Income	100	83	-17

$= C3-B3$ $= C4-B4$

Similarly, you can copy the formula in cell D3 (difference between budgeted and actual sales) to D4 (difference between budgeted and actual interest income).

Excel automatically rewrites the cell references so they refer to the correct cells. You can view a cell's formula by activating the cell and looking in the formula bar near the top of the window.

B6		f_x	=SUM(B3:B5)

	A	B	C	
1	Item Name	Budget	Actual	Dif
2	Income Items			
3	Sales	8200	8103	
4	Interest Income	100	83	
5	Other Income	200	115	
6	Total Income	8500	8301	
7	Expense Items			

C6		f_x	=SUM(C3:C5)

	A	B	C	
1	Item Name	Budget	Actual	Dif
2	Income Items			
3	Sales	8200	8103	
4	Interest Income	100	83	
5	Other Income	200	115	
6	Total Income	8500	8301	
7	Expense Items			

build the budget worksheet

copy and paste

One way to copy formulas is with the Copy and Paste commands.

1 Drag to select cells D3 and E3.

	A	B	C	D	E
1	Item Name	Budget	Actual	Difference % Diff	
2	Income Items				
3	Sales	8200	8103	-97	-0.0[...]83
4	Interest Income	100	83		

2 Click the Copy button in the Clipboard group on the Ribbon's Home tab.

A marquee appears around selected cells.

3 Activate cell D8.

	A	B	C	D	E
1	Item Name	Budget	Actual	Difference % Diff	
2	Income Items				
3	Sales	8200	8103	-97	-0.01183
4	Interest Income	100	83		
5	Other Income	200	115		
6	Total Income	8500			
7	Expense Items				
8	Automobile	150	182		

4 Click the Paste button in the Clipboard group of the Ribbon's Home tab.

The formulas in cells D3 and E3 are copied to cells D8 and E8. The marquee remains around the originally selected cells, indicating that they can be pasted else-where.

	A	B	C	D	E
1	Item Name	Budget	Actual	Difference % Diff	
2	Income Items				
3	Sales	8200	8103	-97	-0.01183
4	Interest Income	100	83		
5	Other Income	200	115		
6	Total Income	8500			
7	Expense Items				
8	Automobile	150	182	32	0.213333
9	Bank Fees	25	25		

5 Activate cell D22.

	A	B	C	D	E
1	Item Name	Budget	Actual	Difference % Diff	
2	Income Items				
3	Sales	8200	8103	-97	-0.01183
4	Interest Income	100	83		
5	Other Income	200	115		
6	Total Income	8500			
7	Expense Items				
8	Automobile	150	182	32	0.213333
9	Bank Fees	25	25		
10	Contributions	30	50		
11	Depreciation	300	300		
12	Insurance	120	120		
13	Interest Expense	75	94		
14	Office Supplies	200	215		
15	Postage	360	427		
16	Professional Fees	180	180		
17	Rent	1200	1200		
18	Repairs	120	245		
19	Taxes	360	365		
20	Telephone	275	209		
21	Travel & Entertainment				
22	Entertainment	500	412		

6 Press Enter. The formulas are copied to cells D22 and E22. The marquee disappears, indicating the selection can no longer be pasted elsewhere.

	A	B	C	D	E
1	Item Name	Budget	Actual	Difference % Diff	
2	Income Items				
3	Sales	8200	8103	-97	-0.01183
4	Interest Income	100	83		
5	Other Income	200	115		
6	Total Income	8500			
7	Expense Items				
8	Automobile	150	182	32	0.213333
9	Bank Fees	25	25		
10	Contributions	30	50		
11	Depreciation	300	300		
12	Insurance	120	120		
13	Interest Expense	75	94		
14	Office Supplies	200	215		
15	Postage	360	427		
16	Professional Fees	180	180		
17	Rent	1200	1200		
18	Repairs	120	245		
19	Taxes	360	365		
20	Telephone	275	209		
21	Travel & Entertainment				
22	Entertainment	500	412	-88	-0.176

Paste Options **button** (see extra bits)

build the budget worksheet

use the fill handle

A quick way to copy the contents of one cell to one or more adjacent cells is with the fill handle. We'll use the fill handle to finish up the worksheet entries.

1 Activate cell B6.

	A	B	C	
1	Item Name	Budget	Actual	[
2	Income Items			
3	Sales	8200	8103	
4	Interest Income	100	83	
5	Other Income	200	115	
6	Total Income	8500		
7	Expense Items			

—— Fill handle

2 Position the mouse pointer on the selection's fill handle—a tiny square in the bottom-right corner of the selection box. The mouse pointer turns into a black cross.

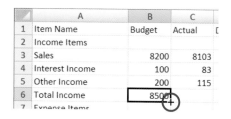

3 Press the mouse button and drag to the right. As you drag, a gray border stretches over the cells you pass over.

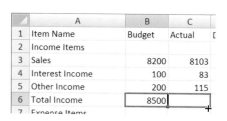

4 When the border surrounds cells B6 and C6, release the mouse button. The formula in cell B6 is copied to cell C6.

	A	B	C	
1	Item Name	Budget	Actual	Diff
2	Income Items			
3	Sales	8200	8103	
4	Interest Income	100	83	
5	Other Income	200	115	
6	Total Income	8500	8301	
7	Expense Items			
8	Automobile	150	182	

Auto Fill Options button ⌐ (see extra bits)

build the budget worksheet

5 Repeat steps 1–4 for cell B27 to copy its formula to C27 and for cell B28 to copy its formula to cell C28. When you're finished, the worksheet should look like this:

	A	B	C	D	E
1	Item Name	Budget	Actual	Difference	% Diff
2	Income Items				
3	Sales	8200	8103	-97	-0.01183
4	Interest Income	100	83		
5	Other Income	200	115		
6	Total Income	8500	8301		
7	Expense Items				
8	Automobile	150	182	32	0.213333
9	Bank Fees	25	25		
10	Contributions	30	50		
11	Depreciation	300	300		
12	Insurance	120	120		
13	Interest Expense	75	94		
14	Office Supplies	200	215		
15	Postage	360	427		
16	Professional Fees	180	180		
17	Rent	1200	1200		
18	Repairs	120	245		
19	Taxes	360	365		
20	Telephone	275	209		
21	Travel & Entertainment				
22	Entertainment	500	412	-88	-0.176
23	Meals	250	342		
24	Travel	600	269		
25	Utilities	800	741		
26	Other Expenses	150	248		
27	Total Expenses	5695	5624		
28	Net Income	2805	2677		
29					

6 Drag to select cells D3 and E3.

	A	B	C	D	E
1	Item Name	Budget	Actual	Difference	% Diff
2	Income Items				
3	Sales	8200	8103	-97	-0.0113
4	Interest Income	100	83		
5	Other Income	200	115		
6	Total Income	8500	8301		
7	Expense Items				

7 Position the mouse pointer on the selection's fill handle.

8 Press the mouse button down and drag so the border completely surrounds cells D3 through E6.

	A	B	C	D	E
1	Item Name	Budget	Actual	Difference	% Diff
2	Income Items				
3	Sales	8200	8103	-97	-0.01183
4	Interest Income	100	83		
5	Other Income	200	115		
6	Total Income	8500	8301		
7	Expense Items				

9 Release the mouse button. The two formulas are copied down to the cells you dragged over.

	A	B	C	D	E
1	Item Name	Budget	Actual	Difference	% Diff
2	Income Items				
3	Sales	8200	8103	-97	-0.01183
4	Interest Income	100	83	-17	-0.17
5	Other Income	200	115	-85	-0.425
6	Total Income	8500	8301	-199	-0.02341
7	Expense Items				

build the budget worksheet

use the fill handle (cont'd)

10 Repeat steps 6–9 to copy cells D8 and E8 to the range beneath it (shown here) and cells D22 and E22 to the range beneath it.

	A	B	C	D	E
1	Item Name	Budget	Actual	Difference	% Diff
2	Income Items				
3	Sales	8200	8103	-97	-0.01183
4	Interest Income	100	83	-17	-0.17
5	Other Income	200	115	-85	-0.425
6	Total Income	8500	8301	-199	-0.02341
7	Expense Items				
8	Automobile	150	182	32	0.213333
9	Bank Fees	25	25		
10	Contributions	30	50		
11	Depreciation	300	300		
12	Insurance	120	120		
13	Interest Expense	75	94		
14	Office Supplies	200	215		
15	Postage	360	427		
16	Professional Fees	180	180		
17	Rent	1200	1200		
18	Repairs	120	245		
19	Taxes	360	365		
20	Telephone	275	209		
21	Travel & Entertainment				
22	Entertainment	500	412	-88	-0.176

When you're finished, the worksheet should look like this.

	A	B	C	D	E
1	Item Name	Budget	Actual	Difference	% Diff
2	Income Items				
3	Sales	8200	8103	-97	-0.01183
4	Interest Income	100	83	-17	-0.17
5	Other Income	200	115	-85	-0.425
6	Total Income	8500	8301	-199	-0.02341
7	Expense Items				
8	Automobile	150	182	32	0.213333
9	Bank Fees	25	25	0	0
10	Contributions	30	50	20	0.666667
11	Depreciation	300	300	0	0
12	Insurance	120	120	0	0
13	Interest Expense	75	94	19	0.253333
14	Office Supplies	200	215	15	0.075
15	Postage	360	427	67	0.186111
16	Professional Fees	180	180	0	0
17	Rent	1200	1200	0	0
18	Repairs	120	245	125	1.041667
19	Taxes	360	365	5	0.013889
20	Telephone	275	209	-66	-0.24
21	Travel & Entertainment				
22	Entertainment	500	412	-88	-0.176
23	Meals	250	342	92	0.368
24	Travel	600	269	-331	-0.55167
25	Utilities	800	741	-59	-0.07375
26	Other Expenses	150	248	98	0.653333
27	Total Expenses	5695	5624	-71	-0.01247
28	Net Income	2805	2677	-128	-0.04563

Have you been saving your work?

Now is a good time to click the Save button on the Quick Access toolbar to save your work up to this point.

build the budget worksheet

change a value

In reviewing this worksheet, I realize that we made an error when entering values. The actual sales amount for the month wasn't 8103 as we entered. It was really 9103! Better enter the correct value now.

1 Activate cell C3.

	A	B	C	D	E
1	Item Name	Budget	Actual	Difference	% Diff
2	Income Items				
3	Sales	8200	8103	-97	-0.01183
4	Interest Income	100	83	-17	-0.17
5	Other Income	200	115	-85	-0.425

2 Type 9103. This new value overwrites the value already entered.

	A	B	C	D	E
1	Item Name	Budget	Actual	Difference	% Diff
2	Income Items				
3	Sales	8200	9103	-97	-0.01183
4	Interest Income	100	83	-17	-0.17
5	Other Income	200	115	-85	-0.425

3 Press Enter.

The value changes, but what's more important is that all of the formulas that referenced that value, either directly or indirectly, also change. Compare the orange highlighted cells in this illustration with the same cells in the illustration on the previous page to see for yourself.

This is the reason we use spreadsheet programs!

	A	B	C	D	E
1	Item Name	Budget	Actual	Difference	% Diff
2	Income Items				
3	Sales	8200	9103	903	0.110122
4	Interest Income	100	83	-17	-0.17
5	Other Income	200	115	-85	-0.425
6	Total Income	8500	9301	801	0.094235
7	Expense Items				
8	Automobile	150	182	32	0.213333
9	Bank Fees	25	25	0	0
10	Contributions	30	50	20	0.666667
11	Depreciation	300	300	0	0
12	Insurance	120	120	0	0
13	Interest Expense	75	94	19	0.253333
14	Office Supplies	200	215	15	0.075
15	Postage	360	427	67	0.186111
16	Professional Fees	180	180	0	0
17	Rent	1200	1200	0	0
18	Repairs	120	245	125	1.041667
19	Taxes	360	365	5	0.013889
20	Telephone	275	209	-66	-0.24
21	Travel & Entertainment				
22	Entertainment	500	412	-88	-0.176
23	Meals	250	342	92	0.368
24	Travel	600	269	-331	-0.55167
25	Utilities	800	741	-59	-0.07375
26	Other Expenses	150	248	98	0.653333
27	Total Expenses	5695	5624	-71	-0.01247
28	Net Income	2805	3677	872	0.310873
29					

extra bits

name the sheet p. 24

- As you'll see in Chapter 8, you can instruct Excel to automatically display a sheet name in a printed report's header or footer. That's a good reason to give a sheet an appropriate name.

activate a cell p. 27

- When you use the point-and-click method for activating a cell, you must click. If you don't click, the cell pointer won't move and the cell you're pointing to won't be activated.

enter row headings p. 28

- When you enter text in a cell, Excel's AutoComplete feature may suggest entries based on previous entries in the column.

To accept an entry, press Enter when it appears. Otherwise, just keep typing what you want to enter. The AutoComplete suggestion will eventually go away.

make a column wider p. 30

- You can't change the width of a single cell. You must change the width of the entire column the cell is in.

enter values pp. 31–32

- You can enter any values you like in this step. But if you enter the same values I do, you can later compare the results of your formulas to mine to make sure the formulas you enter in the next step are correct.

- Do not include currency symbols or commas when entering values. Doing so will apply number formatting. I explain how to format cell contents, including values, in Chapter 6.

- If you use the arrow keys to move from one cell to the next, the selection area disappears. Although you can enter values without a selection area, using a selection area makes it easier to move from one cell to another.

- If, after entering values, you discover that one of the values is incorrect, activate the cell with the incorrect value, enter the correct value, and press Enter to save it.

calculate a difference p. 33

- In Excel, all formulas begin with an equal sign (=).

- Although you can write a formula that subtracts one number from another, using cell references in the formula ensures that the formula's results remain correct, even if referenced cells' values change.

- As our formula is written, if the actual amount is lower than the budgeted amount, the difference appears as a negative number. You can make this appear as a positive number by switching the order of the cell references so the formula is =B3-C3.

calculate a percent diff p. 34

- The number of decimal places that appear in the results of the formula depends on the width of the column the formula is in.

- Don't worry that the percentages Excel calculates don't look like percentages. Later, in Chapter 6, we'll format the worksheet so the numbers look like percentages.

- If the budgeted amount in a cell is 0, the formula for the percent difference will display the error message #DIV/0! Enter this formula in cell E3 to prevent that error: =IF(ISERR(D3/B3),0,D3/B3) This rather complex formula uses logic to determine whether the formula results in an error and, if it does, results in 0.

sum some values pp. 35–36

- The SUM function is probably Excel's most used function. It can be used to add up any range of values.

- Excel is not case-sensitive when evaluating functions. You can type SUM, sum, Sum, or even sUm when you write the formula and Excel will understand.

copy and paste p. 39

- The appearance of the Copy button varies depending on your monitor's screen resolution and the size of the Excel application window. On lower resolution settings or for smaller windows, the button may look like this when you click it:

- The Paste Options button appears when you use the Paste command. Clicking this button displays a menu of options you can use immediately after pasting one or more cells.

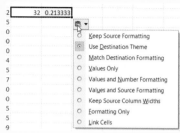

use the fill handle pp. 40–42

- The Auto Fill Options button appears when you use the fill handle to copy formulas. Clicking this button displays a menu of options you can use immediately after filling cells.

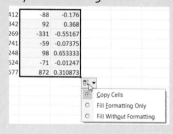

change a value p. 43

- You can use this technique to change any label, value, or formula in a worksheet cell.

- To delete the contents of a cell, activate the cell, press Backspace, and press Enter. Don't use the Spacebar to delete a cell's contents; this merely replaces its contents with a space character.

shortcut keys for this chapter

Copy	Ctrl + C
Paste	Ctrl + V
Save	Ctrl + S

4. duplicate the worksheet

So far, we've created a budget worksheet for one month. Our project, however, includes budget worksheets for three months.

While you could simply repeat the steps in Chapter 3 twice to create two more worksheets, there is a better—and quicker—way. You can duplicate the January worksheet, clear out the values you entered, and enter new values for February. You can then do the same thing for March.

In this chapter, we'll do just that. But just to make things interesting, we'll add and remove a couple of expense categories. As you'll see, this will make the consolidation process in Chapter 5 a bit more challenging.

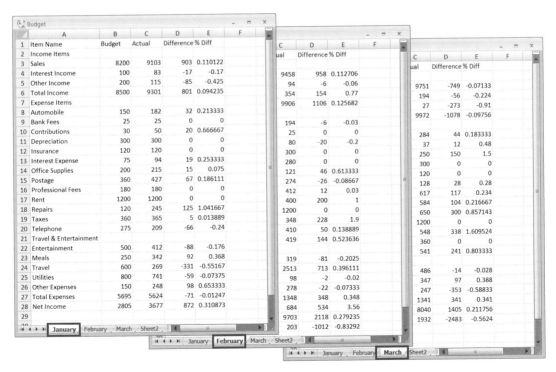

copy the sheet

Excel offers several ways to copy a worksheet. The quickest and easiest way is to drag the sheet tab.

1 Click the tab for the sheet you want to duplicate—in this case, the one we named January— to activate it.

2 Position the mouse pointer on the sheet tab.

3 Hold down the Ctrl key and drag the sheet tab to the right.

As you drag, a tiny page icon with a plus sign in it appears at the mouse pointer and a triangle appears to indicate where the duplicate sheet will appear among the sheet tabs.

4 When the triangle appears between the sheets named January and Sheet2, release the mouse button.

A new sheet named January (2) appears.

5 Repeat steps 1–4 to duplicate the worksheet again, placing the copy between January (2) and Sheet2. The new copy is named January (3).

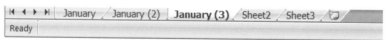

6 Follow the instructions on page 24 to rename January (2) to February and January (3) to March.

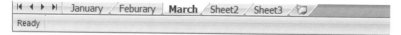

duplicate the worksheet

clear the values

At this point, all three sheets are identical except for their names. We need to clear out the values in the February and March sheets, leaving the labels and formulas, so we can enter new values. Because the two sheets are identical and the values are in the same cells in both sheets, we can clear the values in both sheets at the same time.

1 Click the February tab to activate that sheet.

2 Hold down the Ctrl key and click the March tab.

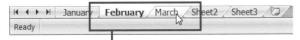

Both tabs become selected (they turn white)...

...and [Group] appears beside the workbook name in the title bar.

3 Position the mouse pointer on cell B3, press the mouse button, and drag down to cell C5 to select all of the cells with income values.

	A	B	C	D	E
1	Item Name	Budget	Actual	Difference	% Diff
2	Income Items				
3	Sales	8200	9103	903	0.110122
4	Interest Income	100	83	-17	-0.17
5	Other Income	200	115	-85	-0.425
6	Total Income	8500	9301	801	0.094235
7	Expense Items				
8	Automobile	150	183	33	0.213333

4 Choose Clear Contents from the Clear menu in the Editing group of the Ribbon's Home tab.

duplicate the worksheet **49**

clear the values (cont'd)

The cells' contents are removed.

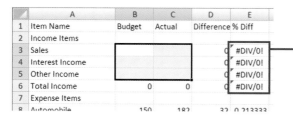

Don't worry about these errors; they'll go away when you fill in new values.

5 Position the mouse pointer on cell B8, press the mouse button, and drag down to cell C26 to select all of the cells with expense values.

6 Choose Clear Contents from the Clear menu in the Editing group of the Ribbon's Home tab (shown on previous page).

The cells' contents are removed.

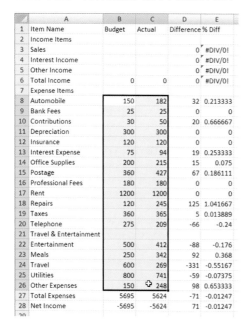

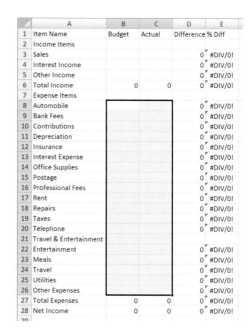

7 Click the January tab to clear the group selection. You can then click the February tab to work with just that worksheet.

duplicate the worksheet

insert a row

February is the month when the big company party is held. Although expenses for this party are part of Entertainment expenses, we want to track the party's budgeted and actual expenses on a separate line. To do this, we need to insert a new row between rows 22 and 23 (Entertainment and Meals).

1 Click the February sheet tab to activate that sheet.

2 Position the mouse pointer on the row heading for row 23. It turns into an arrow pointing to the right.

3 Click once. The entire row becomes selected.

4 Click the Insert button in the Cells group on the Ribbon's Home tab.

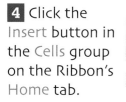

A new row is inserted beneath row 22 and all the rows beneath it shift down.

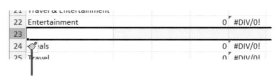

Insert options button
(see Extra Bits)

5 Make sure cell A23 is active—if it isn't, click it.

6 Type Annual Party and press Enter.

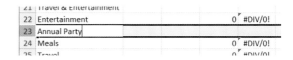

delete a row

The accountant has laid down the law. No more categorizing expenses as Other Expenses. Starting in March, he wants all expenses properly categorized in one of the other existing expense categories. That means we need to delete the row for Other Expenses.

1 Click the March sheet tab to activate that sheet.

2 Position the mouse pointer on the row heading for row 26. It turns into an arrow pointing to the right.

24	Travel
25	Utilities
26	Other Expenses
27	Total Expenses
28	Net Income

3 Click once. The entire row becomes selected.

24	Travel		0	#DIV/0!
25	Utilities		0	#DIV/0!
26	Other Expenses		0	#DIV/0!
27	Total Expenses	0	0	0	#DIV/0!
28	Net Income	0	0	0	#DIV/0!

4 Click the Delete button in the Cells group on the Ribbon's Home tab.

Delete Cells

Delete rows or columns from the table or sheet.

The selected row is deleted and all the rows beneath it shift up.

24	Travel		0	#DIV/0!
25	Utilities		0	#DIV/0!
26	Total Expenses	0	0	0	#DIV/0!
27	Net Income	0	0	0	#DIV/0!
28				

Have you been saving your work?

Now is a good time to click the Save button on the Quick Access toolbar to save your work up to this point.

duplicate the worksheet

enter new values

The February and March worksheets are ready for their values. We'll follow the same basic steps on pages 31–32 to create entry areas and enter the data. To prevent ourselves from accidentally overwriting the formulas in cells B6 and C6, we'll create two separate entry areas for each worksheet.

1 Click the February sheet tab to activate that sheet.

2 Drag from cell B8 to C27 to select that range of cells.

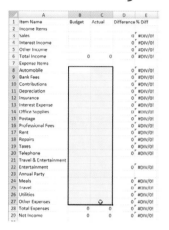

3 Hold down the Ctrl key and drag from cell B3 to C5 to add that range to the selection.

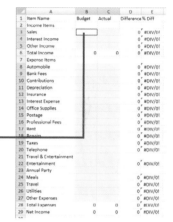

Note that the active cell is the first cell in the second selection.

4 Enter the values shown here in each cell. Be sure to press Enter to advance from one cell to the next. Pay attention; Excel will go through the cells in the top selection before it begins activating cells in the bottom selection.

Excel automatically copies formulas to the blank row when you enter values into it.

	A	B	C	D	E
1	Item Name	Budget	Actual	Difference	% Diff
2	Income Items				
3	Sales	8500	9458	958	0.112706
4	Interest Income	100	94	-6	-0.06
5	Other Income	200	354	154	0.77
6	Total Income	8800	9906	1106	0.125682
7	Expense Items				
8	Automobile	200	194	-6	-0.03
9	Bank Fees	25	25	0	0
10	Contributions	100	80	-20	-0.2
11	Depreciation	300	300	0	0
12	Insurance	280	280	0	0
13	Interest Expense	75	121	46	0.613333
14	Office Supplies	300	274	-26	-0.08667
15	Postage	400	412	12	0.03
16	Professional Fees	200	400	200	1
17	Rent	1200	1200	0	0
18	Repairs	120	348	228	1.9
19	Taxes	360	410	50	0.138889
20	Telephone	275	419	144	0.523636
21	Travel & Entertainment				
22	Entertainment	400	319	-81	-0.2025
23	Annual Party	1800	2513	713	0.396111
24	Meals	100	98	-2	-0.02
25	Travel	300	278	-22	-0.07333
26	Utilities	1000	1348	348	0.348
27	Other Expenses	150	684	534	3.56
28	Total Expenses	7585	9703	2118	0.279235
29	Net Income	1215	203	-1012	-0.83292

enter new values (cont'd)

5 Click the March sheet tab to activate that sheet.

6 Repeat steps 2-4 for cells B8 to C25 and B3 to C5, entering the values shown here.

	A	B	C	D	E
1	Item Name	Budget	Actual	Difference	% Diff
2	Income Items				
3	Sales	10500	9751	-749	-0.07133
4	Interest Income	250	194	-56	-0.224
5	Other Income	300	27	-273	-0.91
6	Total Income	11050	9972	-1078	-0.09756
7	Expense Items				
8	Automobile	240	284	44	0.183333
9	Bank Fees	25	37	12	0.48
10	Contributions	100	250	150	1.5
11	Depreciation	300	300	0	0
12	Insurance	120	120	0	0
13	Interest Expense	100	128	28	0.28
14	Office Supplies	500	617	117	0.234
15	Postage	480	584	104	0.216667
16	Professional Fees	350	650	300	0.857143
17	Rent	1200	1200	0	0
18	Repairs	210	548	338	1.609524
19	Taxes	360	360	0	0
20	Telephone	300	541	241	0.803333
21	Travel & Entertainment				
22	Entertainment	500	486	-14	-0.028
23	Meals	250	347	97	0.388
24	Travel	600	247	-353	-0.58833
25	Utilities	1000	1341	341	0.341
26	Total Expenses	6635	8040	1405	0.211756
27	Net Income	4415	1932	-2483	-0.5624
28					

Have you been saving your work?

Now is a good time to click the Save button on the Quick Access toolbar to save your work up to this point.

duplicate the worksheet

extra bits

copy the sheet p. 48

- I explain how to identify the sheet tab for an active sheet on page 24.
- If you drag a sheet tab without holding down the Ctrl key, you'll change the sheet's position among the sheet tabs rather than copy it.

clear the values pp. 49–50

- Don't believe that you cleared out the contents of two worksheets at once? Click the sheet tabs for February and March to see for yourself!
- It's important to remove the group sheet selection as instructed in step 7 before entering new values in the February worksheet. Otherwise, you'll enter the same values in both the February and March worksheets.

insert a row p. 51

- The Insert button in the Cells group inserts as many rows as you have selected above the selected row(s). So if you select three rows and click this button, Excel will insert three rows above the first selected row.
- If you select a column by clicking on its column heading, you can click the Insert button in the Cells group to insert a column to the left of it.
- The Insert Options button appears immediately after you insert a row, column, or cell. Clicking this button displays a menu of options for formatting the inserted item.

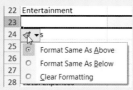

- Excel automatically rewrites formulas as necessary when you insert a row or column.

extra bits (cont'd)

delete a row p. 52

- If you select one or more columns by clicking on or dragging over column headings, you can use the Delete button in the Cells group to delete them.

- Excel automatically rewrites formulas as necessary when you delete a row or column.

shortcut keys for this chapter

Clear Contents	Del
Save	Ctrl + S

5. consolidate the results

We now have three worksheets full of budget and actual information. Our next step is to consolidate this information into one summary worksheet for the quarter. We'll do that with Excel's consolidation feature.

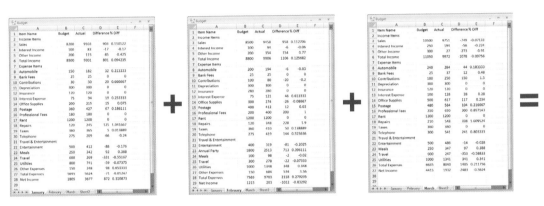

prepare the sheet

The consolidated information will go on its own sheet. We can prepare the sheet by activating it, renaming it, and activating the first cell of the consolidation range.

1 Click the sheet tab for Sheet2 to activate it.

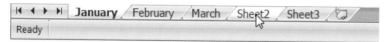

2 Follow the instructions on page 24 to name the sheet tab Quarter 1.

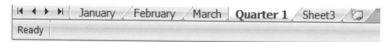

3 Activate cell A1.

consolidate

Excel's consolidation feature uses the Consolidate dialog to collect your consolidation settings, including the worksheet ranges you want to include in the consolidation and the type of consolidation you want to perform.

1 Click the Data tab on the Ribbon.

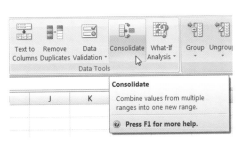

2 Click the Consolidate button in the Data Tools group.

The Consolidate dialog appears.

3 Choose Sum from the Function drop-down list.

4 Turn on all check boxes in the bottom half of the dialog.

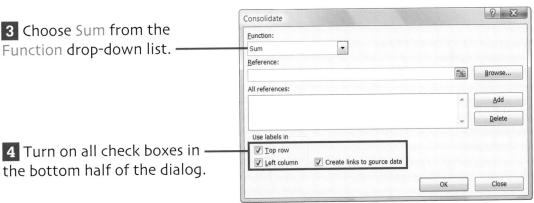

5 Click the January sheet tab so that sheet becomes active behind the dialog. January! appears in the Reference box.

Reference:
January!

consolidate the results

consolidate (cont'd)

6 Position the mouse pointer on cell A1.

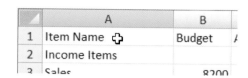

7 Press the mouse button and drag down and to the right to select from cell A1 to cell D28. As you drag, the Consolidate dialog collapses so you can see what you're doing and a selection marquee appears around the cells you drag over.

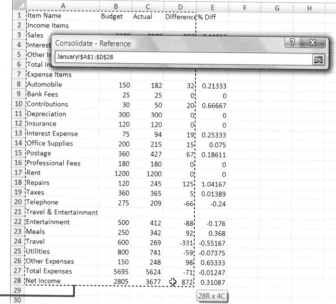

selection
marquee

8 Release the mouse button. The range you selected appears in the Reference box.

Reference:

January!$A$1:$D$28

9 Click Add. The reference is copied to the All references box.

Reference:

January!$A$1:$D$28

All references:

January!$A$1:$D$28

10 Click the February sheet tab to activate that sheet. February!$A$1:$D$28 appears in the Reference box and a selection marquee in the worksheet behind the dialog indicates that range of cells.

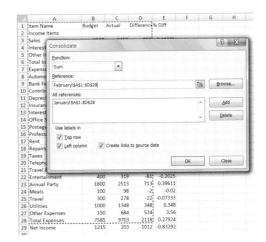

11 Position the mouse pointer on cell A1.

12 Press the mouse button and drag down and to the right to select from cell A1 to cell D29. As you drag, the Consolidate dialog collapses.

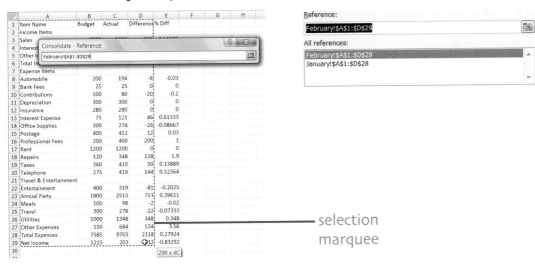

selection marquee

13 Release the mouse button. The range you selected appears in the Reference box.

14 Click Add. The reference is copied to the All references box.

Reference:

February!$A$1:$D$29

All references:

February!$A$1:$D$29
January!$A$1:$D$28

consolidate the results

consolidate (cont'd)

15 Click the March sheet tab so that sheet becomes active. March!$A$1:$D$29 appears in the Reference box and a selection marquee in the worksheet indicates that range of cells.

16 Position the mouse pointer on cell A1.

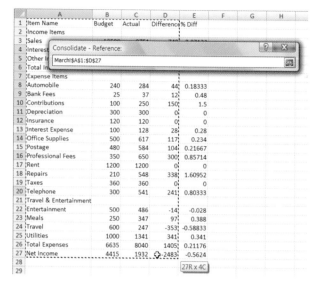

17 Press the mouse button and drag down and to the right to select from cell A1 to cell D27. As you drag, the Consolidate dialog collapses.

18 Release the mouse button. The range you selected appears in the Reference box.

19 Click Add. The reference moves to the All references box.

At this point, the Consolidate dialog should look like this.

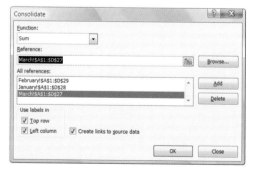

20 Click OK.

Excel creates the consolidation and displays it in the Quarter 1 worksheet.

consolidate the results

check the consolidation

When you consolidate multiple worksheets as instructed here, you create a new worksheet with "3-D" references to the source worksheets. Because Excel has to display contents from all of the source cells, it automatically displays the consolidation as an outline with the outline collapsed so only the total for each category appears.

Double-click the right border of column A's heading to widen the column.

Click an outline symbol to display or hide rows.

Excel enters the name of the source workbook in column B. In this example, all source data is in Budget.

Activate a cell to see its formula in the formula bar. This example shows a reference to a cell in the February worksheet.

Excel places the category total beneath the detail.

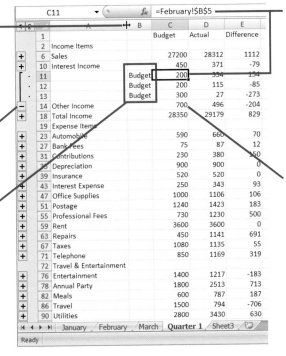

If one of the source worksheets changes, the consolidation automatically changes.

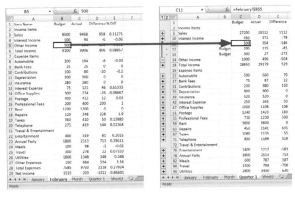

consolidate the results

calculate percent diff

When we created our consolidation, we omitted the percent difference calculation on the source worksheets. The reason: Our consolidation used the SUM function to add values in the source worksheets. Adding the percentages would result in incorrect values for the consolidated percent differences. As a result, we need to recreate the percent difference formula in the consolidation worksheet and copy it to the appropriate cells.

1 Click the sheet tab for the Quarter 1 worksheet to activate that sheet.

2 Enter % Diff in cell F1 and press Enter.

3 Enter the formula = E6/C6 in cell F6. You can either type it in or follow the procedure on page

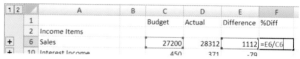

34 to enter the formula by typing and clicking. (If you do click, be sure to click in the correct cells!) Don't forget to press Enter to complete the formula.

4 Use techniques on pages 39–42 to copy the formula to cells F10 to F18, F23 to F71, and F76 to F101.

When you're finished, it should look like this:

Have you been saving your work?

Now is a good time to click the Save button on the Quick Access toolbar to save your work up to this point.

	A	B	C	D	E	F
1			Budget	Actual	Difference	%Diff
2	Income Items					
6	Sales		27200	28312	1112	0.04088
10	Interest Income		450	371	-79	-0.17556
14	Other Income		700	496	-204	-0.29143
18	Total Income		28350	29179	829	0.02924
19	Expense Items					
23	Automobile		590	660	70	0.11864
27	Bank Fees		75	87	12	0.16
31	Contributions		230	380	150	0.65217
35	Depreciation		900	900	0	0
39	Insurance		520	520	0	0
43	Interest Expense		250	343	93	0.372
47	Office Supplies		1000	1106	106	0.106
51	Postage		1240	1423	183	0.14758
55	Professional Fees		730	1230	500	0.68493
59	Rent		3600	3600	0	0
63	Repairs		450	1141	691	1.53556
67	Taxes		1080	1135	55	0.05093
71	Telephone		850	1169	319	0.37529
72	Travel & Entertainment					
76	Entertainment		1400	1217	-183	-0.13071
78	Annual Party		1800	2513	713	0.39611
82	Meals		600	787	187	0.31167
86	Travel		1500	794	-706	-0.47067
90	Utilities		2800	3430	630	0.225
93	Other Expenses		300	932	632	2.10667
97	Total Expenses		19915	23367	3452	0.17334
101	Net Income		8435	5812	-2623	-0.31097

consolidate the results

extra bits

consolidate pp. 59–62

- Because each worksheet in the consolidation has a slightly different organization—remember, we added a row in one and deleted a row in another—you must turn on the Left column check box to properly consolidate. Doing so tells Excel to sum values based on category name (the row label) rather than row position.

calculate percent diff p. 64

- If you use the fill handle to copy the formula in cell F6 to other cells, Excel automatically copies the formula to cells in hidden rows you drag over. This doesn't really matter, though, since we're only interested in the consolidated numbers and will keep the hidden rows hidden.

shortcut keys for this chapter

Save   Ctrl + S

6. format worksheets

Although the information in our four worksheets is accurate and informative, it doesn't look very good. And in this day and age, looks are almost everything. We need to dress these worksheets up to make them more presentable.

Excel offers many extremely flexible formatting options. Our worksheets can benefit from some font and number formatting, as well as alignment, borders, and color. As shown here, we'll transform our plain Jane worksheets into worksheets that demand attention.

On the following pages, I'll show you how to apply formatting to the January worksheet. You can repeat those steps on your own for the other worksheets in our workbook.

Before

After

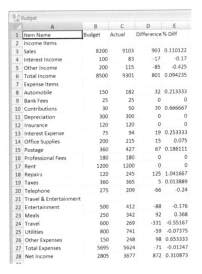

set font formatting

Font formatting changes the way individual characters of text appear. By default, Excel 2007 for Windows Vista uses 11 point Calibri font. You can change the font settings applied to any combination of worksheet cells.

In our worksheets, we'll make the column and row headings bold and larger so they really stand out. We'll also change the font applied to the entire worksheet to something a little more interesting.

1 Drag to select cells A1 to A28.

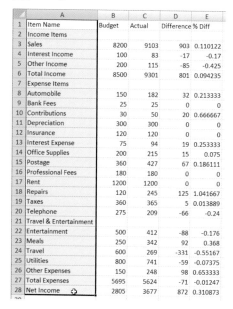

2 Hold down the Ctrl key and drag to add cells B1 to E1 to the selection.

3 Click the Bold button in the Font group of the Ribbon's Home tab.

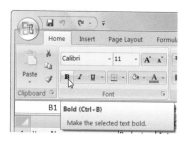

The text in the selected cells turns bold.

	A	B	C	D	E
1	**Item Name**	**Budget**	**Actual**	**Difference**	**% Diff**
2	**Income Items**				
3	**Sales**	8200	9103	903	0.110122
4	Interest Income	100	83	-17	-0.17

4 Choose 12 from the Font Size drop-down list in the Font group of the Ribbon's Home tab.

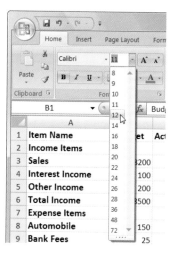

The text in the selected cells gets larger.

	A	B	C	D	E
1	Item Name	Budget	Actual	Differenc	% Diff
2	Income Items				
3	Sales		8200	9103	903	0.110122

5 Click the Select All button in the top corner of the worksheet grid to select all cells in the worksheet.

	A	B	C	D	E
1	Item Name	Budget	Actual	Differenc	% Diff
2	Income Items				
3	Sales	8200	9103	903	0.110122
4	Interest Income	100	83	-17	-0.17
5	Other Income	200	115	-85	-0.425
6	Total Income	8500	9301	801	0.094235
7	Expense Items				
8	Automobile	150	182	32	0.213333
9	Bank Fees	25	25	0	0
10	Contributions	30	50	20	0.666667
11	Depreciation	300	300	0	0
12	Insurance	120	120	0	0
13	Interest Expense	75	94	19	0.253333
14	Office Supplies	200	215	15	0.075
15	Postage	360	427	67	0.186111
16	Professional Fees	180	180	0	0

6 Choose Garamond from the Font drop-down list in the Font group of the Ribbon's Home tab.

The text in the selected cells changes to the Garamond font.

	A	B	C	D	E
1	Item Name	Budget	Actual	Differenc	% Diff
2	Income Items				
3	Sales	8200	9103	903	0.110122
4	Interest Income	100	83	-17	-0.17
5	Other Income	200	115	-85	-0.425
6	Total Income	8500	9301	801	0.0942353
7	Expense Items				
8	Automobile	150	182	32	0.2133333
9	Bank Fees	25	25	0	0
10	Contributions	30	50	20	0.6666667
11	Depreciation	300	300	0	0
12	Insurance	120	120	0	0
13	Interest Expense	75	94	19	0.2533333
14	Office Supplies	200	215	15	0.075
15	Postage	360	427	67	0.1861111
16	Professional Fees	180	180	0	0

format worksheets

format values

The dollar amounts in our worksheets would be a lot easier to read with commas and dollar signs.

1 Drag to select cells B3 to D28.

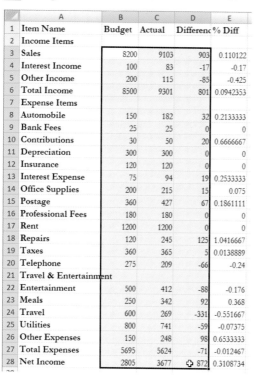

	A	B	C	D	E
1	Item Name	Budget	Actual	Difference	% Diff
2	Income Items				
3	Sales	8200	9103	903	0.110122
4	Interest Income	100	83	-17	-0.17
5	Other Income	200	115	-85	-0.425
6	Total Income	8500	9301	801	0.0942353
7	Expense Items				
8	Automobile	150	182	32	0.2133333
9	Bank Fees	25	25	0	0
10	Contributions	30	50	20	0.6666667
11	Depreciation	300	300	0	0
12	Insurance	120	120	0	0
13	Interest Expense	75	94	19	0.2533333
14	Office Supplies	200	215	15	0.075
15	Postage	360	427	67	0.1861111
16	Professional Fees	180	180	0	0
17	Rent	1200	1200	0	0
18	Repairs	120	245	125	1.0416667
19	Taxes	360	365	5	0.0138889
20	Telephone	275	209	-66	-0.24
21	Travel & Entertainment				
22	Entertainment	500	412	-88	-0.176
23	Meals	250	342	92	0.368
24	Travel	600	269	-331	-0.551667
25	Utilities	800	741	-59	-0.07375
26	Other Expenses	150	248	98	0.6533333
27	Total Expenses	5695	5624	-71	-0.012467
28	Net Income	2805	3677	872	0.3108734

2 Click the Comma Style button in the Number group of the Ribbon's Home tab.

Comma Style
Display the value of the cell with a thousands separator.

This will change the format of the cell to Accounting without a currency symbol.

Commas, decimal places, and parentheses (for negative numbers) appear, as needed, for all values in selected cells.

	A	B	C	D	E
1	Item Name	Budget	Actual	Difference	% Diff
2	Income Items				
3	Sales	8,200.00	9,103.00	903.00	0.110122
4	Interest Income	100.00	83.00	(17.00)	-0.17
5	Other Income	200.00	115.00	(85.00)	-0.425
6	Total Income	8,500.00	9,301.00	801.00	0.0942353
7	Expense Items				
8	Automobile	150.00	182.00	32.00	0.2133333
9	Bank Fees	25.00	25.00	-	0
10	Contributions	30.00	50.00	20.00	0.6666667
11	Depreciation	300.00	300.00	-	0
12	Insurance	120.00	120.00	-	0
13	Interest Expense	75.00	94.00	19.00	0.2533333
14	Office Supplies	200.00	215.00	15.00	0.075
15	Postage	360.00	427.00	67.00	0.1861111
16	Professional Fees	180.00	180.00	-	0
17	Rent	1,200.00	1,200.00	-	0
18	Repairs	120.00	245.00	125.00	1.0416667
19	Taxes	360.00	365.00	5.00	0.0138889
20	Telephone	275.00	209.00	(66.00)	-0.24
21	Travel & Entertainment				
22	Entertainment	500.00	412.00	(88.00)	-0.176
23	Meals	250.00	342.00	92.00	0.368
24	Travel	600.00	269.00	(331.00)	-0.551667
25	Utilities	800.00	741.00	(59.00)	-0.07375
26	Other Expenses	150.00	248.00	98.00	0.6533333
27	Total Expenses	5,695.00	5,624.00	(71.00)	-0.012467
28	Net Income	2,805.00	3,677.00	872.00	0.3108734

format worksheets

3 Drag to select cells B3 to D3, B6 to D6, B8 to D8, and B27 to D28. Remember you must hold down the Ctrl key to select multiple ranges.

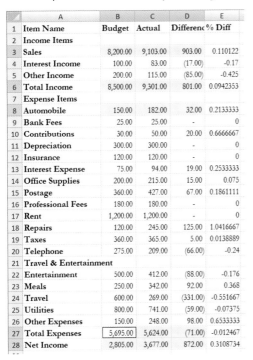

	A	B	C	D	E
1	Item Name	Budget	Actual	Difference	% Diff
2	Income Items				
3	Sales	8,200.00	9,103.00	903.00	0.110122
4	Interest Income	100.00	83.00	(17.00)	-0.17
5	Other Income	200.00	115.00	(85.00)	-0.425
6	Total Income	8,500.00	9,301.00	801.00	0.0942353
7	Expense Items				
8	Automobile	150.00	182.00	32.00	0.2133333
9	Bank Fees	25.00	25.00	-	0
10	Contributions	30.00	50.00	20.00	0.6666667
11	Depreciation	300.00	300.00	-	0
12	Insurance	120.00	120.00	-	0
13	Interest Expense	75.00	94.00	19.00	0.2533333
14	Office Supplies	200.00	215.00	15.00	0.075
15	Postage	360.00	427.00	67.00	0.1861111
16	Professional Fees	180.00	180.00	-	0
17	Rent	1,200.00	1,200.00	-	0
18	Repairs	120.00	245.00	125.00	1.0416667
19	Taxes	360.00	365.00	5.00	0.0138889
20	Telephone	275.00	209.00	(66.00)	-0.24
21	Travel & Entertainment				
22	Entertainment	500.00	412.00	(88.00)	-0.176
23	Meals	250.00	342.00	92.00	0.368
24	Travel	600.00	269.00	(331.00)	-0.551667
25	Utilities	800.00	741.00	(59.00)	-0.07375
26	Other Expenses	150.00	248.00	98.00	0.6533333
27	Total Expenses	5,695.00	5,624.00	(71.00)	-0.012467
28	Net Income	2,805.00	3,677.00	872.00	0.3108734

4 Click the Accounting Number Format button in the Number group of the Ribbon's Home tab.

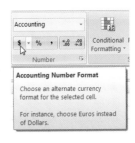

Accounting

Conditional Formatting

Number

Accounting Number Format

Choose an alternate currency format for the selected cell.

For instance, choose Euros instead of Dollars.

Currency symbols appear beside values in the selected cells.

	A	B	C	D	E
1	Item Name	Budget	Actual	Difference	% Diff
2	Income Items				
3	Sales	$8,200.00	$9,103.00	$ 903.00	0.110122
4	Interest Income	100.00	83.00	(17.00)	-0.17
5	Other Income	200.00	115.00	(85.00)	-0.425
6	Total Income	$8,500.00	$9,301.00	$ 801.00	0.0942353
7	Expense Items				
8	Automobile	$ 150.00	$ 182.00	$ 32.00	0.2133333
9	Bank Fees	25.00	25.00	-	0
10	Contributions	30.00	50.00	20.00	0.6666667
11	Depreciation	300.00	300.00	-	0
12	Insurance	120.00	120.00	-	0
13	Interest Expense	75.00	94.00	19.00	0.2533333
14	Office Supplies	200.00	215.00	15.00	0.075
15	Postage	360.00	427.00	67.00	0.1861111
16	Professional Fees	180.00	180.00	-	0
17	Rent	1,200.00	1,200.00	-	0
18	Repairs	120.00	245.00	125.00	1.0416667
19	Taxes	360.00	365.00	5.00	0.0138889
20	Telephone	275.00	209.00	(66.00)	-0.24
21	Travel & Entertainment				
22	Entertainment	500.00	412.00	(88.00)	-0.176
23	Meals	250.00	342.00	92.00	0.368
24	Travel	600.00	269.00	(331.00)	-0.551667
25	Utilities	800.00	741.00	(59.00)	-0.07375
26	Other Expenses	150.00	248.00	98.00	0.6533333
27	Total Expenses	$5,695.00	$5,624.00	$ (71.00)	-0.012467
28	Net Income	$2,805.00	$3,677.00	$ 872.00	0.3108734

format percentages

We can also use number formatting to format the percentages in column E so they look like percentages.

1 Drag to select all cells E3 to E28.

	A	B	C	D	E
1	Item Name	Budget	Actual	Difference	% Diff
2	Income Items				
3	Sales	$8,200.00	$9,103.00	$ 903.00	0.110122
4	Interest Income	100.00	83.00	(17.00)	-0.17
5	Other Income	200.00	115.00	(85.00)	-0.425
6	Total Income	$8,500.00	$9,301.00	$ 801.00	0.0942353
7	Expense Items				
8	Automobile	$ 150.00	$ 182.00	$ 32.00	0.2133333
9	Bank Fees	25.00	25.00	-	0
10	Contributions	30.00	50.00	20.00	0.6666667
11	Depreciation	300.00	300.00	-	0
12	Insurance	120.00	120.00	-	0
13	Interest Expense	75.00	94.00	19.00	0.2533333
14	Office Supplies	200.00	215.00	15.00	0.075
15	Postage	360.00	427.00	67.00	0.1861111
16	Professional Fees	180.00	180.00	-	0
17	Rent	1,200.00	1,200.00	-	0
18	Repairs	120.00	245.00	125.00	1.0416667
19	Taxes	360.00	365.00	5.00	0.0138889
20	Telephone	275.00	209.00	(66.00)	-0.24
21	Travel & Entertainment				
22	Entertainment	500.00	412.00	(88.00)	-0.176
23	Meals	250.00	342.00	92.00	0.368
24	Travel	600.00	269.00	(331.00)	-0.551667
25	Utilities	800.00	741.00	(59.00)	-0.07375
26	Other Expenses	150.00	248.00	98.00	0.6533333
27	Total Expenses	$5,695.00	$5,624.00	$ (71.00)	-0.012467
28	Net Income	$2,805.00	$3,677.00	$ 872.00	0.3108734

2 Click the Percent Style button in the Number group of the Ribbon's Home tab.

The numbers are formatted as percentages without any decimal places.

	A	B	C	D	E
1	Item Name	Budget	Actual	Difference	% Diff
2	Income Items				
3	Sales	$8,200.00	$9,103.00	$ 903.00	11%
4	Interest Income	100.00	83.00	(17.00)	-17%
5	Other Income	200.00	115.00	(85.00)	-43%
6	Total Income	$8,500.00	$9,301.00	$ 801.00	9%
7	Expense Items				
8	Automobile	$ 150.00	$ 182.00	$ 32.00	21%
9	Bank Fees	25.00	25.00	-	0%
10	Contributions	30.00	50.00	20.00	67%
11	Depreciation	300.00	300.00		0%

3 Click the Increase Decimal button in the Number group of the Ribbon's Home tab.

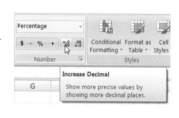

The numbers are reformatted so there's one decimal place.

	A	B	C	D	E
1	Item Name	Budget	Actual	Difference	% Diff
2	Income Items				
3	Sales	$8,200.00	$9,103.00	$ 903.00	11.0%
4	Interest Income	100.00	83.00	(17.00)	-17.0%
5	Other Income	200.00	115.00	(85.00)	-42.5%
6	Total Income	$8,500.00	$9,301.00	$ 801.00	9.4%
7	Expense Items				
8	Automobile	$ 150.00	$ 182.00	$ 32.00	21.3%
9	Bank Fees	25.00	25.00	-	0.0%
10	Contributions	30.00	50.00	20.00	66.7%
11	Depreciation	300.00	300.00		0.0%

format worksheets

set column widths

When you create a worksheet, Excel automatically sets a default width for columns: 8.11 characters (or 80 pixels).

We've already used the AutoFit feature to increase the width of column A so its text fits in the column. And you may have noticed that Excel widened one or two columns to accommodate the number formatting we applied.

Now we'll make column A a little wider again—remember, we increased the text size and applied bold formatting which made the text take up more space. We'll also set the width of columns B, C, D, and E to a consistent wider setting.

1 Double-click the right border of column A.

	A	B
1	Item Name	Budget
2	Income Items	
3	Sales	$8,200.00
4	Interest Income	100.00
5	Other Income	200.00
6	Total Income	$8,500.00
7	Expense Items	
8	Automobile	$ 150.00
9	Bank Fees	25.00
10	Contributions	30.00
11	Depreciation	300.00
12	Insurance	120.00
13	Interest Expense	75.00
14	Office Supplies	200.00
15	Postage	360.00
16	Professional Fees	180.00
17	Rent	1,200.00
18	Repairs	120.00
19	Taxes	360.00
20	Telephone	275.00
21	Travel & Entertainment	
22	Entertainment	500.00
23	Meals	250.00

The column automatically widens again to accommodate the widest text in the column.

	A	B
1	Item Name	Budget
2	Income Items	
3	Sales	$8,200.00
4	Interest Income	100.00
5	Other Income	200.00
6	Total Income	$8,500.00
7	Expense Items	
8	Automobile	$ 150.00
9	Bank Fees	25.00
10	Contributions	30.00
11	Depreciation	300.00
12	Insurance	120.00
13	Interest Expense	75.00
14	Office Supplies	200.00
15	Postage	360.00
16	Professional Fees	180.00
17	Rent	1,200.00
18	Repairs	120.00
19	Taxes	360.00
20	Telephone	275.00
21	Travel & Entertainment	
22	Entertainment	500.00
23	Meals	250.00

2 Position the mouse pointer on the column heading for column B. It turns into an arrow pointing down.

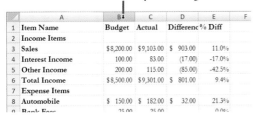

	A	B	C	D	E	F
1	Item Name	Budget	Actual	Difference	% Diff	
2	Income Items					
3	Sales	$8,200.00	$9,103.00	$ 903.00	11.0%	
4	Interest Income	100.00	83.00	(17.00)	-17.0%	
5	Other Income	200.00	115.00	(85.00)	-42.5%	
6	Total Income	$8,500.00	$9,301.00	$ 801.00	9.4%	
7	Expense Items					
8	Automobile	$ 150.00	$ 182.00	$ 32.00	21.3%	
9	Bank Fees	25.00	25.00		0.0%	

3 Press the mouse button and drag to the right to select columns B, C, D, and E.

	A	B	C	D	E	4C	F
1	Item Name	Budget	Actual	Difference	% Diff		
2	Income Items						
3	Sales	$8,200.00	$9,103.00	$ 903.00	11.0%		
4	Interest Income	100.00	83.00	(17.00)	-17.0%		
5	Other Income	200.00	115.00	(85.00)	-42.5%		
6	Total Income	$8,500.00	$9,301.00	$ 801.00	9.4%		
7	Expense Items						
8	Automobile	$ 150.00	$ 182.00	$ 32.00	21.3%		
9	Bank Fees	25.00	25.00		0.0%		

set column widths (cont'd)

4 Choose Column Width from the Format menu in the Cells group of the Ribbon's Home tab.

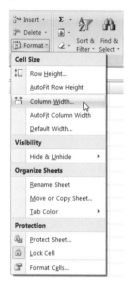

The Column Width dialog appears.

5 Enter 12 in the text box and click OK.

The columns widen.

	A	B	C	D	E
1	Item Name	Budget	Actual	Difference	% Diff
2	Income Items				
3	Sales	$ 8,200.00	$ 9,103.00	$ 903.00	11.0%
4	Interest Income	100.00	83.00	(17.00)	-17.0%
5	Other Income	200.00	115.00	(85.00)	-42.5%
6	Total Income	$ 8,500.00	$ 9,301.00	$ 801.00	9.4%
7	Expense Items				
8	Automobile	$ 150.00	$ 182.00	$ 32.00	21.3%
9	Bank Fees	25.00	25.00	-	0.0%

Save your work.

Now is a good time to click the Save button on the Quick Access toolbar to save your work up to this point.

format worksheets

set alignment

By default, text is left-aligned in a cell and a number (including a date or time) is right-aligned in a cell. For our worksheet, the headings at the top of columns B, C, D, and E might look better if they were centered.

1 Drag to select cells B1 through E1.

2 Click the Center button in the Alignment group of the Ribbon's Home tab.

The cell contents are centered between the cell's left and right boundaries.

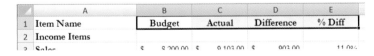

indent text

Entertainment, Meals, and Travel are three row headings that are part of the major Travel & Entertainment category of expenses. We can make that clear to the people who view the worksheet by indenting those three row headings.

1 Select cells A22 through A24.

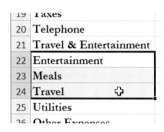

2 Click the Increase Indent button in the Alignment group of the Ribbon's Home tab twice.

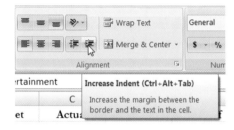

Each selected cell's contents are shifted to the right.

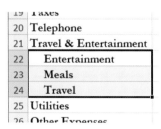

format worksheets

add borders

Borders above and below the totals and net amounts would really help them stand out. We'll add single lines above and below Income and Expense totals and a double line beneath the Net Income amounts.

1 Select cells B6 to E6, and B27 to E27. Remember, you must hold down the Control key to select multiple ranges.

	A	B	C	D	E
1	Item Name	Budget	Actual	Difference	% Diff
2	Income Items				
3	Sales	$ 8,200.00 $	9,103.00 $	903.00	11.0%
4	Interest Income	100.00	83.00	(17.00)	-17.0%
5	Other Income	200.00	115.00	(85.00)	-42.5%
6	Total Income	$ 8,500.00 $	9,301.00 $	801.00	9.4%
7	Expense Items				
8	Automobile	$ 150.00 $	182.00 $	32.00	21.3%
9	Bank Fees	25.00	25.00	-	0.0%
10	Contributions	30.00	50.00	20.00	66.7%
11	Depreciation	300.00	300.00	-	0.0%
12	Insurance	120.00	120.00	-	0.0%
13	Interest Expense	75.00	94.00	19.00	25.3%
14	Office Supplies	200.00	215.00	15.00	7.5%
15	Postage	360.00	427.00	67.00	18.6%
16	Professional Fees	180.00	180.00	-	0.0%
17	Rent	1,200.00	1,200.00	-	0.0%
18	Repairs	120.00	245.00	125.00	104.2%
19	Taxes	360.00	365.00	5.00	1.4%
20	Telephone	275.00	209.00	(66.00)	-24.0%
21	Travel & Entertainment				
22	Entertainment	500.00	412.00	(88.00)	-17.6%
23	Meals	250.00	342.00	92.00	36.8%
24	Travel	600.00	269.00	(331.00)	-55.2%
25	Utilities	800.00	741.00	(59.00)	-7.4%
26	Other Expenses	150.00	248.00	98.00	65.3%
27	Total Expenses	$ 5,695.00 $	5,624.00 $	(71.00)	-1.2%
28	Net Income	$ 2,805.00 $	3,677.00 $	872.00	31.1%

2 Choose Top and Bottom Border from the Borders menu in the Font group of the Ribbon's Home tab.

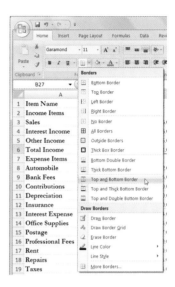

Borders are applied to the top and bottom of all selected cells.

	A	B	C	D	E
1	Item Name	Budget	Actual	Difference	% Diff
2	Income Items				
3	Sales	$ 8,200.00 $	9,103.00 $	903.00	11.0%
4	Interest Income	100.00	83.00	(17.00)	-17.0%
5	Other Income	200.00	115.00	(85.00)	-42.5%
6	Total Income	$ 8,500.00 $	9,301.00 $	801.00	9.4%
7	Expense Items				
8	Automobile	$ 150.00 $	182.00 $	32.00	21.3%
9	Bank Fees	25.00	25.00	-	0.0%
10	Contributions	30.00	50.00	20.00	66.7%
11	Depreciation	300.00	300.00	-	0.0%
12	Insurance	120.00	120.00	-	0.0%
13	Interest Expense	75.00	94.00	19.00	25.3%
14	Office Supplies	200.00	215.00	15.00	7.5%
15	Postage	360.00	427.00	67.00	18.6%
16	Professional Fees	180.00	180.00	-	0.0%
17	Rent	1,200.00	1,200.00	-	0.0%
18	Repairs	120.00	245.00	125.00	104.2%
19	Taxes	360.00	365.00	5.00	1.4%
20	Telephone	275.00	209.00	(66.00)	-24.0%
21	Travel & Entertainment				
22	Entertainment	500.00	412.00	(88.00)	-17.6%
23	Meals	250.00	342.00	92.00	36.8%
24	Travel	600.00	269.00	(331.00)	-55.2%
25	Utilities	800.00	741.00	(59.00)	-7.4%
26	Other Expenses	150.00	248.00	98.00	65.3%
27	Total Expenses	$ 5,695.00 $	5,624.00 $	(71.00)	-1.2%
28	Net Income	$ 2,805.00 $	3,677.00 $	872.00	31.1%

add borders (cont'd)

3 Select cells B28 to E28.

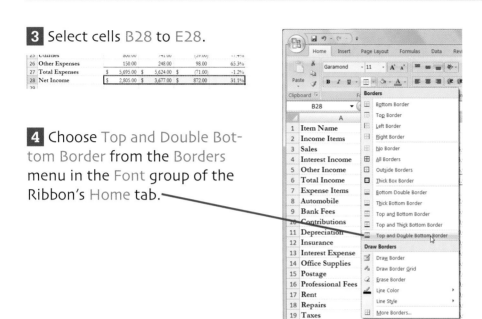

4 Choose Top and Double Bottom Border from the Borders menu in the Font group of the Ribbon's Home tab.

A double border appears beneath the selected cells.

Here's what it should look like when you're done, with the selection area removed:

	A	B	C	D	E
1	Item Name	Budget	Actual	Difference	% Diff
2	Income Items				
3	Sales	$ 8,200.00	$ 9,103.00	$ 903.00	11.0%
4	Interest Income	100.00	83.00	(17.00)	-17.0%
5	Other Income	200.00	115.00	(85.00)	-42.5%
6	Total Income	$ 8,500.00	$ 9,301.00	$ 801.00	9.4%
7	Expense Items				
8	Automobile	$ 150.00	$ 182.00	$ 32.00	21.3%
9	Bank Fees	25.00	25.00	-	0.0%
10	Contributions	30.00	50.00	20.00	66.7%
11	Depreciation	300.00	300.00	-	0.0%
12	Insurance	120.00	120.00	-	0.0%
13	Interest Expense	75.00	94.00	19.00	25.3%
14	Office Supplies	200.00	215.00	15.00	7.5%
15	Postage	360.00	427.00	67.00	18.6%
16	Professional Fees	180.00	180.00	-	0.0%
17	Rent	1,200.00	1,200.00	-	0.0%
18	Repairs	120.00	245.00	125.00	104.2%
19	Taxes	360.00	365.00	5.00	1.4%
20	Telephone	275.00	209.00	(66.00)	-24.0%
21	Travel & Entertainment				
22	Entertainment	500.00	412.00	(88.00)	-17.6%
23	Meals	250.00	342.00	92.00	36.8%
24	Travel	600.00	269.00	(331.00)	-55.2%
25	Utilities	800.00	741.00	(59.00)	-7.4%
26	Other Expenses	150.00	248.00	98.00	65.3%
27	Total Expenses	$ 5,695.00	$ 5,624.00	$ (71.00)	-1.2%
28	Net Income	$ 2,805.00	$ 3,677.00	$ 872.00	31.1%

format worksheets

apply shading

Shading can also improve the appearance of a worksheet. We'll apply dark colored shading to worksheet cells containing headings so they really stand out, then apply a lighter color shading to the rest of the worksheet.

1 Select cells A1 to E1 and A2 to A28. Remember, you must hold down the Control key to select multiple ranges.

	A	B	C	D	E
1	Item Name	Budget	Actual	Difference	% Diff
2	Income Items				
3	Sales	$ 8,200.00	$ 9,103.00	$ 903.00	11.0%
4	Interest Income	100.00	83.00	(17.00)	-17.0%
5	Other Income	200.00	115.00	(85.00)	-42.5%
6	Total Income	$ 8,500.00	$ 9,301.00	$ 801.00	9.4%
7	Expense Items				
8	Automobile	$ 150.00	$ 182.00	$ 32.00	21.3%
9	Bank Fees	25.00	25.00	-	0.0%
10	Contributions	30.00	50.00	20.00	66.7%
11	Depreciation	300.00	300.00	-	0.0%
12	Insurance	120.00	120.00	-	0.0%
13	Interest Expense	75.00	94.00	19.00	25.3%
14	Office Supplies	200.00	215.00	15.00	7.5%
15	Postage	360.00	427.00	67.00	18.6%
16	Professional Fees	180.00	180.00	-	0.0%
17	Rent	1,200.00	1,200.00	-	0.0%
18	Repairs	120.00	245.00	125.00	104.2%
19	Taxes	360.00	365.00	5.00	1.4%
20	Telephone	275.00	209.00	(66.00)	-24.0%
21	Travel & Entertainment				
22	Entertainment	500.00	412.00	(88.00)	-17.6%
23	Meals	250.00	342.00	92.00	36.8%
24	Travel	600.00	269.00	(331.00)	-55.2%
25	Utilities	800.00	741.00	(59.00)	-7.4%
26	Other Expenses	150.00	248.00	98.00	65.3%
27	Total Expenses	$ 5,695.00	$ 5,624.00	(71.00)	-1.2%
28	Net Income	$ 2,805.00	$ 3,677.00	872.00	31.1%

2 Choose a dark color from the Fill Color menu in the Font group of the Ribbon's Home tab.

The color is applied to selected cells. Here's what the top bunch of cells might look like with the selection area removed.

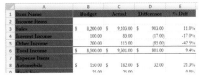

3 Select cells B2 to E28.

	A	B	C	D	E
1	Item Name	Budget	Actual	Difference	% Diff
2	Income Items				
3	Sales	$ 8,200.00	$ 9,103.00	$ 903.00	11.0%
4	Interest Income	100.00	83.00	(17.00)	-17.0%
5	Other Income	200.00	115.00	(85.00)	-42.5%
6	Total Income	$ 8,500.00	$ 9,301.00	$ 801.00	9.4%
7	Expense Items				
8	Automobile	$ 150.00	$ 182.00	$ 32.00	21.3%
9	Bank Fees	25.00	25.00	-	0.0%
10	Contributions	30.00	50.00	20.00	66.7%
11	Depreciation	300.00	300.00	-	0.0%
12	Insurance	120.00	120.00	-	0.0%
13	Interest Expense	75.00	94.00	19.00	25.3%
14	Office Supplies	200.00	215.00	15.00	7.5%
15	Postage	360.00	427.00	67.00	18.6%
16	Professional Fees	180.00	180.00	-	0.0%
17	Rent	1,200.00	1,200.00	-	0.0%
18	Repairs	120.00	245.00	125.00	104.2%
19	Taxes	360.00	365.00	5.00	1.4%
20	Telephone	275.00	209.00	(66.00)	-24.0%
21	Travel & Entertainment				
22	Entertainment	500.00	412.00	(88.00)	-17.6%
23	Meals	250.00	342.00	92.00	36.8%
24	Travel	600.00	269.00	(331.00)	-55.2%
25	Utilities	800.00	741.00	(59.00)	-7.4%
26	Other Expenses	150.00	248.00	98.00	65.3%
27	Total Expenses	$ 5,695.00	$ 5,624.00	(71.00)	-1.2%
28	Net Income	$ 2,805.00	$ 3,677.00	872.00	31.1%

4 Choose a light color from the Fill Color menu in the Font group of the Ribbon's Home tab.

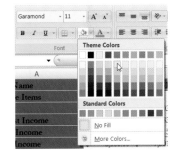

The color is applied to selected cells.

	A	B	C	D	E
1	Item Name	Budget	Actual	Difference	% Diff
2	Income Items				
3	Sales	$ 8,200.00	$ 9,103.00	$ 903.00	11.0%
4	Interest Income	100.00	83.00	(17.00)	-17.0%
5	Other Income	200.00	115.00	(85.00)	-42.5%
6	Total Income	$ 8,500.00	$ 9,301.00	$ 801.00	9.4%
7	Expense Items				
8	Automobile	$ 150.00	$ 182.00	32.00	21.3%

change text color

When we applied dark shading to the worksheet's headings, we created a problem: The black text may not be legible with the dark cell shading. We can fix this problem by making the heading text a lighter color.

1 Select cells A1 to E1 and A2 to A28. Remember, you must hold down the Control key to select multiple ranges.

2 Choose a light color from the Font Color menu in the Font group of the Ribbon's Home tab.

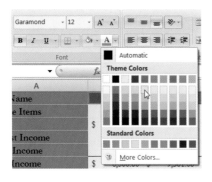

The color is applied to the font characters in selected cells. Here's what the worksheet might look like with the selection area removed.

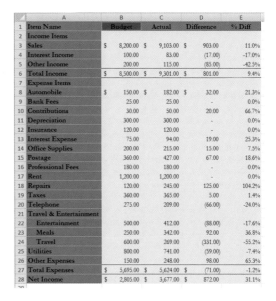

	A	B	C	D	E
1	Item Name	Budget	Actual	Difference	% Diff
2	Income Items				
3	Sales	$ 8,200.00	$ 9,103.00	$ 903.00	11.0%
4	Interest Income	100.00	83.00	(17.00)	-17.0%
5	Other Income	200.00	115.00	(85.00)	-42.5%
6	Total Income	$ 8,500.00	$ 9,301.00	$ 801.00	9.4%
7	Expense Items				
8	Automobile	$ 150.00	$ 182.00	$ 32.00	21.3%
9	Bank Fees	25.00	25.00	-	0.0%
10	Contributions	30.00	50.00	20.00	66.7%
11	Depreciation	300.00	300.00	-	0.0%
12	Insurance	120.00	120.00	-	0.0%
13	Interest Expense	75.00	94.00	19.00	25.3%
14	Office Supplies	200.00	215.00	15.00	7.5%
15	Postage	360.00	427.00	67.00	18.6%
16	Professional Fees	180.00	180.00	-	0.0%
17	Rent	1,200.00	1,200.00	-	0.0%
18	Repairs	120.00	245.00	125.00	104.2%
19	Taxes	360.00	365.00	5.00	1.4%
20	Telephone	275.00	209.00	(66.00)	-24.0%
21	Travel & Entertainment				
22	Entertainment	500.00	412.00	(88.00)	-17.6%
23	Meals	250.00	342.00	92.00	36.8%
24	Travel	600.00	269.00	(331.00)	-55.2%
25	Utilities	800.00	741.00	(59.00)	-7.4%
26	Other Expenses	150.00	248.00	98.00	65.3%
27	Total Expenses	$ 5,695.00	$ 5,624.00	$ (71.00)	-1.2%
28	Net Income	$ 2,805.00	$ 3,677.00	$ 872.00	31.1%

format worksheets

format all worksheets

So far, all we've done is format one of the four worksheets in our workbook file: January. You can follow the steps on pages 68-80 to apply the same formatting to the other worksheets in the file: February, March, and Quarter 1.

Here are a few things to keep in mind:

- To activate a worksheet, click its sheet tab.

- Not all worksheets have the same number of columns and rows, so you won't be able to use the cell selections exactly as written in this chapter. Be sure to select the correct areas when applying formatting.

- In the February worksheet, Annual Party should be indented with the other Travel & Entertainment row headings.

- For the Quarter 1 worksheet, keep the consolidation's detail hidden. You can also hide column B by setting its column width to 0 (zero).

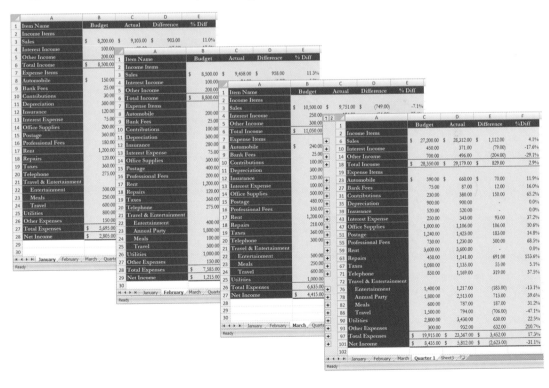

extra bits

set font formatting pp. 68–69

- A font is basically a typeface.

- A point is a unit of measurement roughly equal to 1/72 of an inch. Fonts are measured in points. The bigger the point size, the bigger the characters.

- As you move the mouse pointer over items in the Font menu, the currently highlighted font is temporarily applied to selected cells. This makes it easy to preview what the cells will look like with that font applied.

- Another way to change the font or font size is to type a font name in the Font box (shown here) or value in the Font Size box and press Enter.

- Choose your font carefully! Some fonts are designed for display purposes only and can be difficult to read.

- Don't get carried away with font formatting. Too much formatting can distract the reader.

- Want more font formatting options? Click the Dialog Box Launcher button in the lower-right corner of the Font group on the Ribbon's Home tab.

Then use the Font tab of the Format Cells dialog that appears to set font formatting options and click OK to apply them to selected cells.

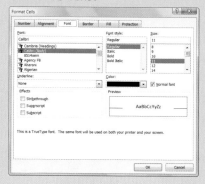

format worksheets

format values pp. 70–71

- Another way to apply number formatting is with the Number Format menu in the Number group of the Ribbon's Home tab.

- For more number formatting options, click the Dialog Box Launcher button in the lower-right corner of the Number group in the Ribbon's Home tab. Set options in the Number tab of the Format Cells dialog and click OK to apply formatting.

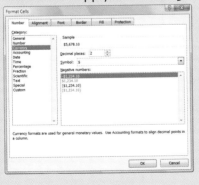

set column widths pp. 73–74

- Another way to change the width of a column is to drag the right edge of its column heading to the left or right.

- You can hide a column by setting its width to 0 (zero) or by selecting it and choosing Hide Columns from the Hide & Unhide submenu on the Format menu in the Home tab's Cells group. To unhide a column, select the columns on either side of it and choose Unhide Columns from the Hide & Unhide submenu on the Format menu in the Home tab's Cells group.

extra bits (cont'd)

set alignment p. 75

- Depending on column width settings, you may find that column headings look better when right-aligned over the numbers beneath them rather than centered. Click the Align Right button in the Alignment group of the Ribbon's Home tab to try it and decide for yourself.

add borders p. 77–78

- Don't confuse borders with underlines. Underlines are part of a cell's font formatting and, when applied, appear only beneath characters in a cell. Borders appear for the entire width of the cell.

- Don't confuse cell gridlines with borders, either. Gray cell gridlines appear onscreen to help you see cell boundaries. Normally, they don't print—although you can elect to print them in the Page Setup dialog. Cell borders always print.

apply shading p. 79

- Although colored shading looks great onscreen and in color printouts, it doesn't always look good in black and white printouts, which turn the colors to shades of gray. If you plan to print in black and white, you may want to minimize dark colored shading in your document.

- Another way to apply shading is with Excel's predefined styles. Choose one of the options in the Cell Styles menu in the Styles group of the Ribbon's Home tab. The benefit of applying styles is that they automatically change text to a contrasting color if necessary.

shortcut keys for this chapter

Bold	Ctrl + B
Percent Style	Ctrl + Shift + %
Increase Indent	Ctrl + Alt + Tab
Save	Ctrl + S

format worksheets

7. add a chart

Excel includes a powerful and flexible charting feature that enables you to create charts based on worksheet information. Its chart formatting commands and options make it easy to create charts to your specifications. Best of all, if any of the data in a source worksheet changes, the chart automatically changes accordingly.

In Excel, charts can be inserted into a workbook file in two ways:

- A chart sheet, as discussed in Chapter 2 and shown below, displays a chart on a separate workbook sheet.

- An embedded chart is a chart that is added as a graphic object to a worksheet.

In this chapter, we'll create a pie chart of actual expenses for the quarter as a separate sheet within our Budget workbook file.

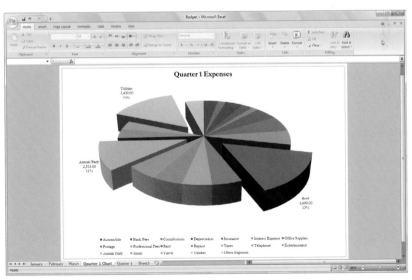

hide a row

Our chart will include all expense categories from the Quarter 1 file. Before we select the information to chart, however, we'll hide the row labeled Travel & Entertainment, which has no values, so it does not appear in the chart.

1 Click the Quarter 1 sheet tab to activate that sheet.

3 Choose Hide Rows from the Hide & Unhide submenu under the Format menu in the Cells group of the Ribbon's Home tab.

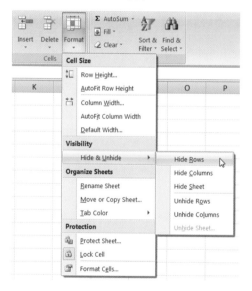

2 Click on the row heading number for row 72 to select it.

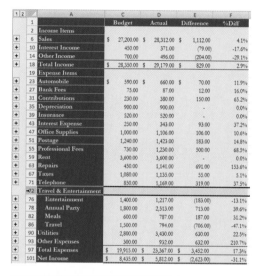

The row disappears.

add a chart

insert a chart

The first step in creating a chart is to select the information you want to include in the chart. This includes both values and corresponding labels. Then choose an option to insert the type of chart you want.

1 Select cells A23 to A93 and cells D23 to D93. Remember, you must hold down the Control key to select multiple ranges.

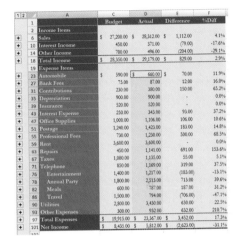

2 Click the Insert tab on the Ribbon.

3 Choose the first 3-D Pie option from the Pie button in the Chart group.

The Chart Tools appear on the Ribbon when a chart is selected.

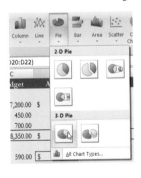

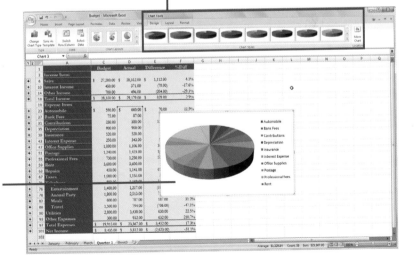

A pie chart appears in its own frame in the worksheet window.

create a chart sheet

To create a chart sheet, you must move an existing chart to its own sheet.

Selection handles indicate that the chart is selected.

1 Click anywhere inside the chart to select the chart and display the Chart Tools on the Ribbon (as shown on the previous page).

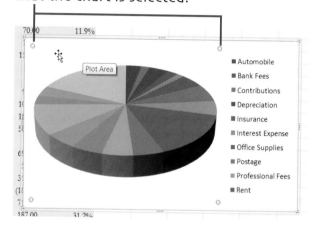

2 Click the Move Chart button in the Location group on the Design tab.

The Move Chart dialog appears.

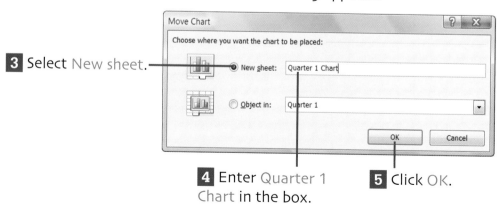

3 Select New sheet.

4 Enter Quarter 1 Chart in the box.

5 Click OK.

add a chart

The chart is moved to its own sheet in the workbook.

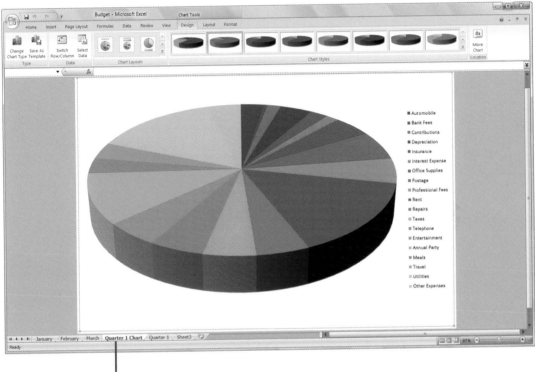

You can click the chart's
sheet tab to view it.

Save your work.

Click the Save button on the
Quick Access toolbar to save
your work up to this point.

add a chart

add a chart title

Although the chart sheet has a name, it doesn't have a title that will appear on the sheet. Let's add one.

1 If necessary, click anywhere in the chart sheet to select it and display the Chart Tools on the Ribbon.

2 Click the Layout tab on the Ribbon.

3 Choose Above Chart from the Chart Title menu in the Labels group of the Ribbon's Layout tab.

The words Chart Title appear in a selected box at the top of the chart sheet.

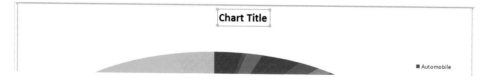

4 Double-click to select the text in the box.

5 Type Quarter 1 Expenses.

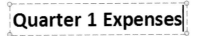

6 Click anywhere else in the chart sheet to accept the text you typed and deselect the title box.

The chart sheet should look like this when you're done:

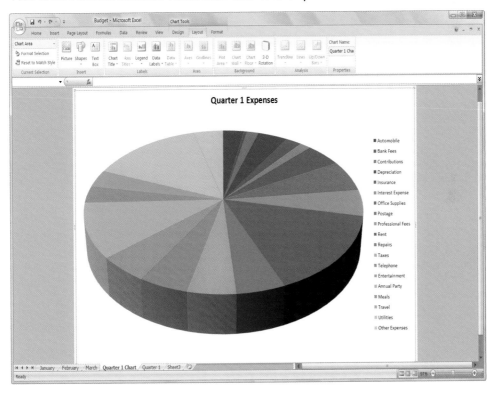

move the legend

To give the chart sheet a more symetrical appearance, let's move the legend to the bottom of the chart.

1 If necessary, select the chart to display the Chart Tools on the Ribbon, then click the Layout tab.

2 Choose Show Legend at Bottom from the Legend menu in the Labels group of the Ribbon's Layout tab.

The legend shifts so it appears at the bottom of the chart.

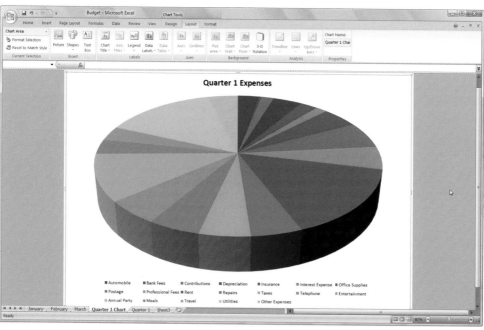

add a chart

explode a pie

You can make one or more pieces of a pie chart really stand out by "exploding" them away from the pie. In our example, we'll emphasize the pie pieces that represent the top three expense items: Rent, Utilities, and Annual Party.

1 Click the piece of pie representing Rent. (You'll know you have the right one when "Rent" appears in its tooltip.) The entire pie chart becomes selected.

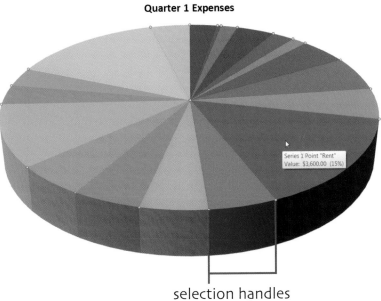

Quarter 1 Expenses

Series 1 Point "Rent"
Value: $3,600.00 (15%)

selection handles

2 Click the pie piece so selection handles appear around it.

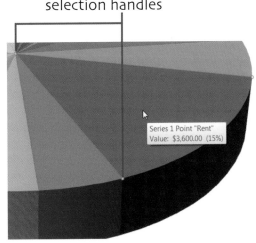

Series 1 Point "Rent"
Value: $3,600.00 (15%)

explode a pie (cont'd)

3 Drag the piece of pie away from the center of the pie. An outline of the pie moves as you drag.

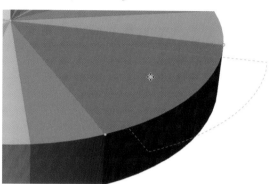

4 Release the mouse button. The pie is redrawn with the piece you dragged "exploded" away.

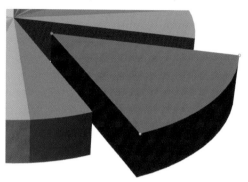

5 Repeat steps 2 through 4 for the pie pieces representing Utilities and Annual Party.

When you're finished, the pie chart should look like this:

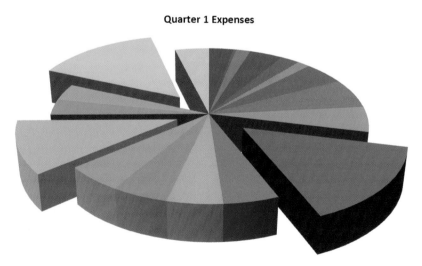

Quarter 1 Expenses

add a chart

add data labels

Data labels provide information about data in a chart. Although this chart includes a color-coded legend, we'll provide additional information about the three biggest expenses using data labels.

1 Click the pie piece for Rent. If the entire chart becomes selected, click it again so only the Rent piece is selected.

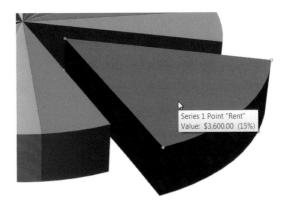

Series 1 Point "Rent"
Value: $3,600.00 (15%)

2 If necessary, click the Layout tab on the Ribbon.

3 Choose Outside End from the Data Labels menu in the Labels group of the Ribbon's Layout tab.

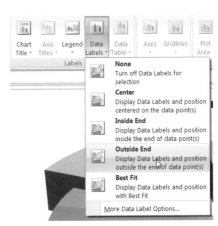

The pie piece value appears at the wide end of the pie piece.

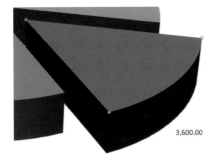

3,600.00

4 Click the data label you created to select it.

3,600.00

Series 1 Point "Rent" Data Label

add data labels (cont'd)

5 Click the data label again so its name, Series 1 Point, "Rent" Data Label, appears in the Chart Elements drop-down list in the Current Selection group of the Ribbon's Layout tab.

6 Click the Format Selection button in the Current Selection group of the Ribbon's Layout tab.

The Format Data Label dialog appears.

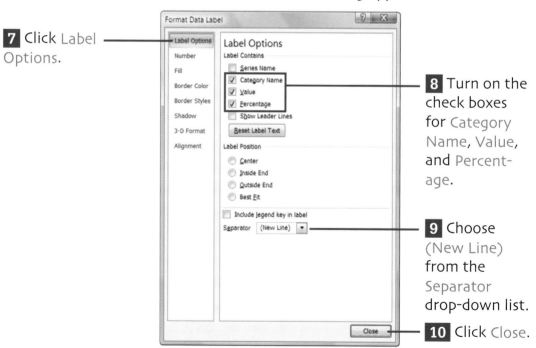

7 Click Label Options.

8 Turn on the check boxes for Category Name, Value, and Percentage.

9 Choose (New Line) from the Separator drop-down list.

10 Click Close.

add a chart

The formatted data label should look like this:

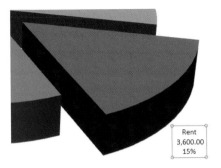

11 Repeat steps 1 through 10 for Utilities and Annual Party.

When you're finished, the pie chart should look like this:

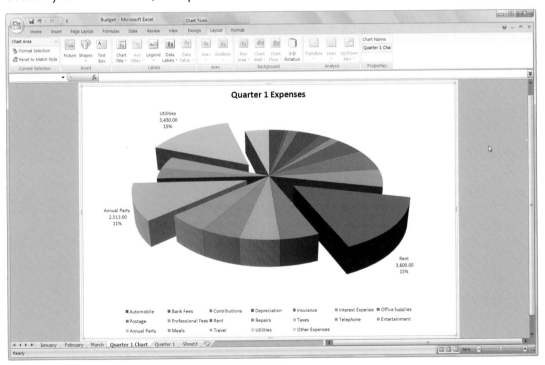

add a chart

format chart text

Since the rest of the workbook uses Garamond as its font, let's change the text in the chart to match it.

1 If necessary, click the Ribbon's Layout tab to display its options.

2 Choose Chart Area from the Chart Elements drop-down list in the Current Selection group of the Ribbon's Layout tab.

3 Click the Ribbon's Home tab.

4 Choose Garamond from the Font drop-down list in the Font group.

The font of all text characters on the chart change to Garamond.

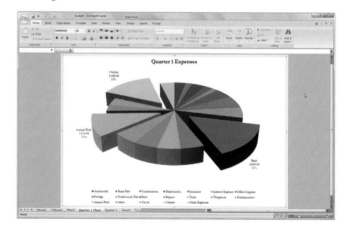

Save your work.

Click the Save button on the Quick Access toolbar to save your work up to this point.

add a chart

extra bits

insert a chart p. 87

- You can move a chart inserted on a worksheet by dragging its border. As you drag, an outline of the chart moves (see below). When you release the mouse button, the chart moves.

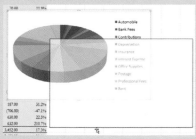

- Choosing All Chart Types from the Pie menu in the Charts group dislays the Insert Chart dialog, which you can use to insert any type of chart.

add a chart title p. 90–91

- You can move a chart title by selecting it and dragging its border. When you release the mouse button, it appears in the new position.

move the legend p. 92

- The position of a chart's legend will impact the size of the chart. You can see this for yourself by trying different Legend options.

explode a pie pp. 93–94

- Exploding a pie may make the pie smaller. The farther out you drag a piece of pie, the smaller the pie may become.

extra bits (cont'd)

add data labels pp. 95–97

- If you wanted data labels to appear for all pieces of the pie, select the entire pie (rather than just one piece) in step 1. Then, when setting options, make sure Series 1 appears in the Chart Element drop-down list in step 5.

- You can move a data label by selecting it and dragging its border. When you release the mouse button, it appears in the new position.

format chart text p. 98

- To format just some of the text in a chart, select the text you want to format and apply formatting with the Home tab's Font group commands.

add a chart

8. share your work

In many instances, when you're finished creating and formatting a worksheet or chart, you'll need to print it or e-mail it to another Excel user.

Although you can just use the Print command to send a sheet to your printer for hard copy, Excel offers a wide variety of page setup options you can use to customize your printout. For example, you can change page orientation and scaling, set margins, and add headers and footers. All of these settings affect the way your sheet will appear when printed.

Fortunately, Excel's Print Preview feature (shown here) enables you to see what your sheets will look like before you print them, so you can fine-tune their appearance without wasting a lot of paper.

This chapter explores many of Excel's page setup options to prepare our worksheets for printing and then to print them. It also explains how you can use Excel and Outlook together to send Excel worksheets to others via e-mail.

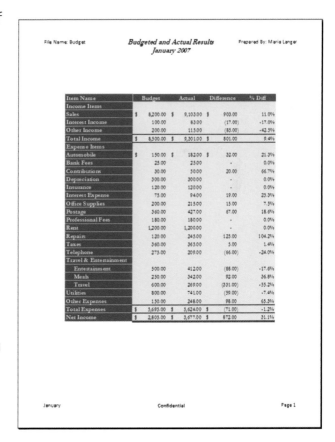

switch to page layout

Throughout this project, we've been working in Normal view, which displays each worksheet as a single scrolling page. Page Layout view, however, displays the worksheet in individual pages, as they will print. It also enables you to set options such as headers and footers.

1 If necessary, click one of the worksheet tabs to display a worksheet.

2 Click the Ribbon's View tab.

3 Click the Page Layout View button in the Workbook Views group.

The current worksheet (and all other worksheets in the workbook file) switches to Page Layout view.

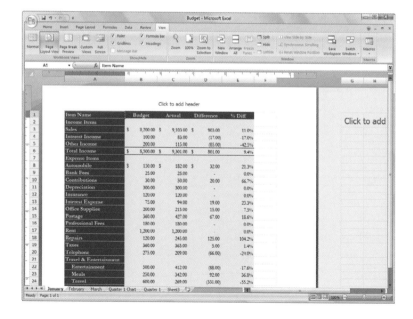

share your work

select the sheets

To print a sheet or set print options for it, you must activate it. Because our workbook includes several worksheets which will all have the same settings, we can select them all and set options for all of them at once.

1 Click the sheet tab for the January sheet.

2 Hold down the Control key and click the sheet tabs for the February, March, and Quarter 1 sheets.

All of the sheet tabs you clicked become selected.

open page setup

The Page Setup dialog is a gold mine of options for setting up worksheets and charts for printing. Its options are organized into five categories:

- Page options control page orientation and scaling.

- Margins options control margin measurements and the centering of the sheet on the page.

- Header/Footer options enable you to choose from predefined headers or footers or create your own.

- Sheet options (which appear for worksheets only) enable you to specify what prints and how it prints or Chart options (which appear for chart sheets only) enable you to specify how a chart will print.

This chapter explores some of these options. But first, let's open that dialog.

1 Click the Page Layout tab on the Ribbon.

2 Click the Dialog Box Launcher button in the bottom-right corner of the Page Setup group in the Ribbon's Page Layout tab.

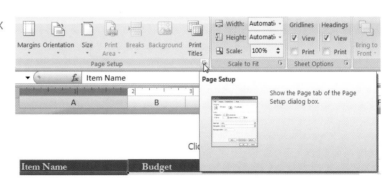

share your work

set page options

Page options affect page orientation and scaling, as well as a few other settings. We'll set Page options for Portrait orientation, 100% scaling, and Letter size paper. These options should be set by default, but we'll check them, just in case they aren't.

1 In the Page Setup dialog, click the Page tab.

2 Select Portrait.

3 Select Adjust to and enter 100 in the box.

4 Choose Letter from the Paper size drop-down list.

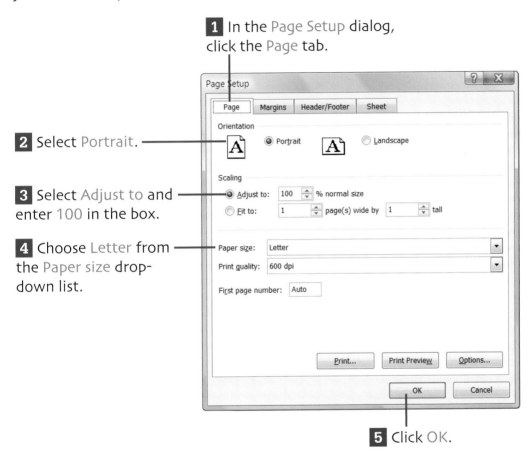

5 Click OK.

adjust margins

A margin is the amount of space between the printable area on a page and the edge of the paper. In Excel, Margins options enable you to control the space between the edge of the paper and the sheet contents, as well as the header or footer. Margins settings also enable you to center a sheet horizontally or vertically on a page.

1 In the Page Setup dialog, click the Margins tab.

2 Enter 2 in the Top box.

3 Enter 1.5 in the Bottom box.

4 Turn on the Horizontally check box.

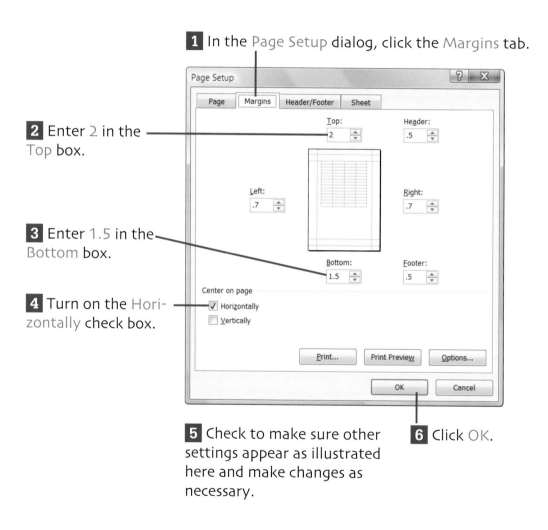

5 Check to make sure other settings appear as illustrated here and make changes as necessary.

6 Click OK.

share your work

add a standard footer

A footer is text that appears at the bottom of every page. In Excel, you add a footer with the Header/Footer options of the Page Setup dialog, which gives you a choice of predefined or custom headers and footers. For our example, we'll add a standard, predefined footer.

1 In the Page Setup dialog, click the Header/Footer tab.

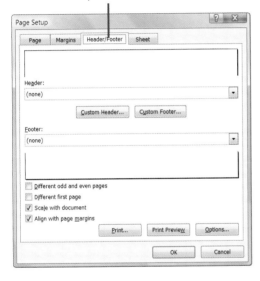

2 Choose January, Confidential, Page 1 from the drop-down list under Footer.

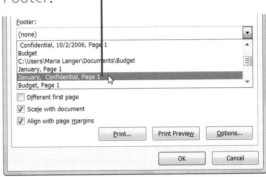

The footer appears in the Footer preview area.

add a custom header

A header is text that appears at the top of every page. In Excel, you add a header with the Header/Footer options of the Page Setup dialog, which gives you a choice of predefined or custom headers and footers. For our example, we'll add a custom header.

1 In the Page Setup dialog, click the Header/Footer tab.

2 Click the Custom Header button.

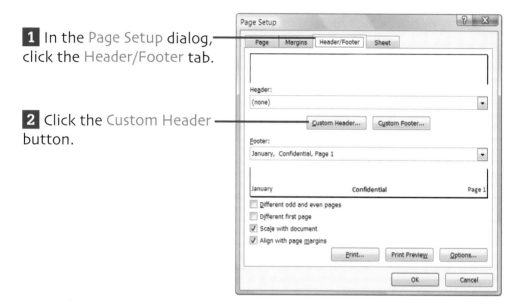

The Header dialog appears.

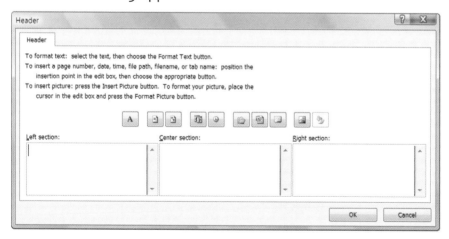

3 In the Left section box, type File Name.

4 Click the Insert File Name button. &[File] should appear.

Left section:

> File Name: &[File]

5 In the Center section box, type Budgeted and Actual Results and press Enter.

6 Click the Insert Sheet Name button. &[Tab] should appear on the next line.

Center section:

> Budgeted and Actual Results
> &[Tab] 2007

7 Press the Spacebar and type 2007.

8 In the Right section box, type Prepared By: and type your name.

Right section:

> Prepared By: Maria Langer

At this point, the Header dialog should look like this.

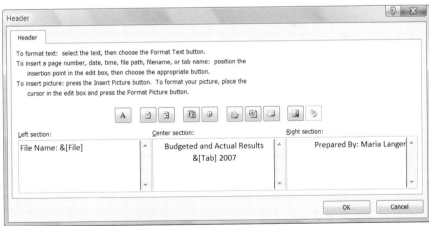

To format text: select the text, then choose the Format Text button.
To insert a page number, date, time, file path, filename, or tab name: position the insertion point in the edit box, then choose the appropriate button.
To insert picture: press the Insert Picture button. To format your picture, place the cursor in the edit box and press the Format Picture button.

Left section:	Center section:	Right section:
File Name: &[File]	Budgeted and Actual Results &[Tab] 2007	Prepared By: Maria Langer

OK   Cancel

9 Select the contents of the Center section box.

Center section:

> Budgeted and Actual Results
> &[Tab] 2007

share your work

add custom header (cont'd)

10 Click the Format Text button.

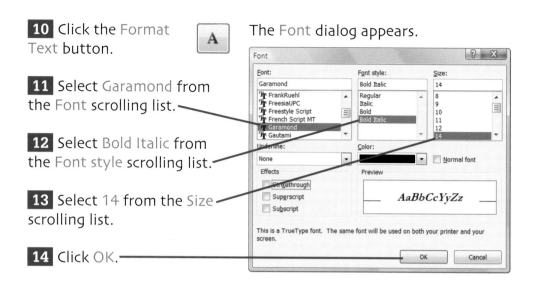

11 Select Garamond from the Font scrolling list.

12 Select Bold Italic from the Font style scrolling list.

13 Select 14 from the Size scrolling list.

14 Click OK.

The Font dialog appears.

The Center section text is formatted to your specifications.

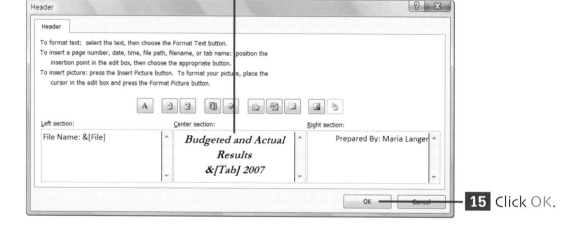

15 Click OK.

Your custom header appears in the Header preview area.

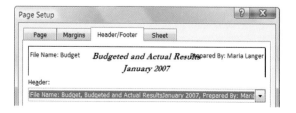

save settings

We've made a bunch of changes in the Page Setup dialog. It's time to save them.

In the Page Setup dialog, click OK.

The settings you made in the dialog are applied to the selected sheets.

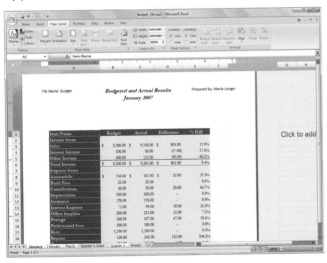

Save your work.

Click the Save button on the Quick Access toolbar to save your work up to this point.

preview the sheets

Excel's Print Preview feature saves time and paper by enabling you to see what a document will look like on paper without actually printing it. If it looks good, you can click a Print button to send it to your printer. If it doesn't look good, you can click a Setup button to go back to the Page Setup dialog and fix it.

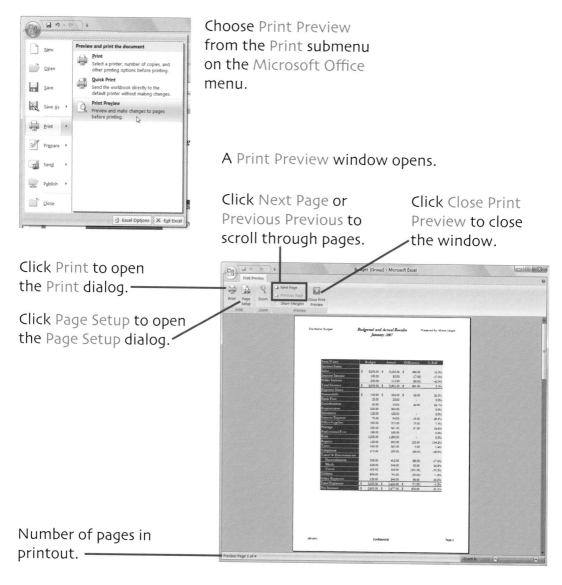

Choose Print Preview from the Print submenu on the Microsoft Office menu.

A Print Preview window opens.

Click Next Page or Previous Previous to scroll through pages.

Click Close Print Preview to close the window.

Click Print to open the Print dialog.

Click Page Setup to open the Page Setup dialog.

Number of pages in printout.

print your work

Once you're satisfied that the worksheets will look good on paper, you can print them.

1 Click Print on the Microsoft Office menu …

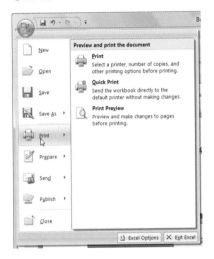

… or, in the Print Preview window (see page 112), click the Print button in the Print group.

The Print dialog appears.

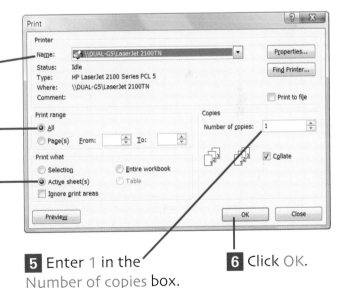

2 Choose a printer from the Name drop-down list.

3 Select All in the Print range area.

4 Select Active sheet(s) in the Print what area.

5 Enter 1 in the Number of copies box.

6 Click OK.

The worksheets are sent to the printer where they print.

send via e-mail

If you're using Excel in a workplace environment, you might find it useful to share your workbook with other Excel users. Excel's E-mail command makes it easy to attach your workbook file to an e-mail message so you can send it to anyone.

1 Click the Save button on the Quick Access toolbar to save your work.

2 Choose E-mail from the Send submenu on the Microsoft Office menu.

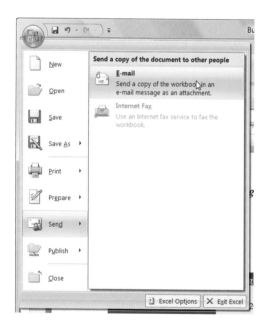

share your work

Excel starts your default e-mail program (in my case, Microsoft Outlook 2007) and displays a new message form with your worksheet attached.

6 Click Send.

The name of the attachment appears here.

3 Enter the e-mail address of the recipient in the To field.

4 If desired, change the subject of the message.

5 Enter the body of the message in this box.

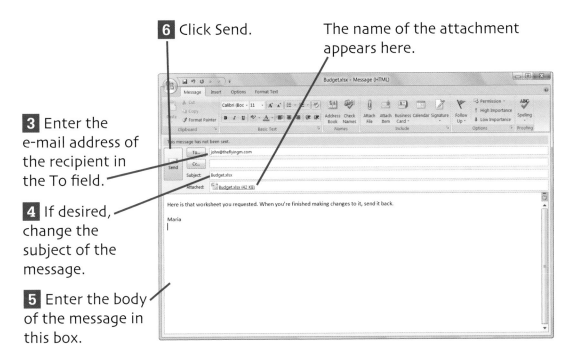

The message with its attachment is sent via e-mail to its recipient.

extra bits

set page options p. 105

- You can also set page margins, print orientation, and paper size using menus in the Page Setup group of the Ribbon's Page Layout tab. Just choose from the available options on the menus there. Keep in mind that the Page Setup dialog offers complete control over all of these options and more.

- If you discover, when previewing your worksheet, that it doesn't quite fit on a single page, you can force it to fit on that page. Select Fit to in the Page options of the Page Setup dialog and make sure 1 is entered in both boxes beside it.

add a standard footer p. 107

- Excel gets your name and company name from information you entered when you installed Excel or the Microsoft Office package.

add a custom header pp. 108–110

- Excel left-aligns the Left section text, centers the Center section text, and right-aligns the Right section text.

- It isn't necessary to enter text in all three sections of a custom header or footer. Just use the sections you need.

- You can also create a custom header in Page Layout view. Just click in the header area to select it and enter the text you want to appear.

save settings p. 111

- Page Setup options are automatically saved with a workbook file when you save the workbook. So once you've set options for a file, you don't have to reset them unless you want to change them.

print your work p. 113

- Clicking the Properties button in the Print dialog displays additional options that are specific to your printer. Consult the manual that came with your printer for additional information about these options.

send via e-mail pp. 114–115

- To send an Excel workbook file to someone who uses an older version of Excel, first save it as an Excel 97-2003 workbook file. Choose Excel 97-2003 Workbook from the Save As submenu on the Microsoft Office menu. Then use the Save As dialog to save a copy of the workbook with a different name and send that file via e-mail.

- Microsoft Excel 2007 can open and work with files created with previous versions of Excel, so you should have no trouble working with files you get from other Excel users.

- If Outlook is not your default e-mail program, consult that program's onscreen help or other documentation to learn more about using it to send messages with attachments.

share your work

index

= (equal sign), formulas, 45

A

Above Chart command, 90

Accounting Number Format button, 71

active cells, 5

addresses, budget worksheets, 25

alignment, formatting worksheets, 75, 84

Alignment group
  Center button, 75
  Increase Indent button, 76

Auto Fill Options button, 40

AutoComplete feature, 44

AutoFit feature, 73

AutoSum button, 35

B

Bold shortcut keys, 84

borders, formatting worksheets, 77–78, 84

Browse Folders button, 21

budget worksheets, 23
  calculations
    differences, 33, 45

net income, 37
percent differences, 34, 45

cells
  activating, 27, 44
  fill handles, 40–42, 46

columns
  entering headings, 29
  making wider, 30, 44

entering information, 26

formulas
  Copy and Paste commands, 39, 45
  copying, 38

naming, 24, 44

references, 25

rows
  AutoComplete feature, 44
  entering headings, 28

values
  changing, 43, 46
  entering, 31–32, 44
  SUM function, 35–36, 45

C

calculations
  differences, 33, 45
  net income, 37

index

percent differences, 34, 45, 64–65

Calibri font, 68

cells

    activating, 27, 44

    budget worksheets, 23

    copying formulas, 38

    fill handles, 40–42, 45

    pointers, 5

    worksheet references, 25

Cells group, 86

Center button, 75

chart sheets, 17, 85, 88–89

Chart Tools tab, 9, 87

charts, 85

    adding titles, 90–91, 99

    creating chart sheets, 88–89

    data labels, 95–97, 100

    exploding pie, 93–94, 99

    formatting text, 98, 100

    hiding row, 86

    inserting, 87, 99

    moving legend, 92, 99

    sharing, 101

        adjusting margins, 106

        custom headers, 108–110, 116

        e-mail, 114–115, 117

        footers, 107, 116

        Page Setup dialog, 104

        Print Preview feature, 112

        printing, 113, 117

        save settings, 111, 116

        setting page options, 105, 116

        sheet selection, 103

        switching to Page Layout view, 102

check boxes, 9, 12

Clear Contents command, 49

Clear Contents shortcut keys, 56

clearing values, duplicating worksheets, 49–50

clicking mouse, 3

Clipboard group, 39

Column Width command, 74

Column Width dialog, 74

columns

    budget worksheets, 23

    formatting widths, 73–74, 83

    headings, 5, 29

    making wider, 30, 44

    worksheet references, 25

Comma Style button, 70

commands

    contextual menu, 11

    menus, 10

    Ribbon, 8, 15

    submenu, 11

Consolidate button, 59

Consolidate dialog, 59–62

consolidating worksheets, 57, 65

    calculating percent differences, 64–65

checking, 63

Consolidate dialog, 59–62

sheet preparation, 58

contextual menus, 11

Copy button, 39

Copy command, formulas, 39

Copy shortcut keys, 46

copying

cells, fill content, 46

duplicate worksheets, 48, 55

formulas, 38

cross pointers, mouse, 3

currency symbols

entering values, 44

formatting worksheets, 71

Current Selection group, 96

Custom Header button, 108

D

data labels, charts, 95–97, 100

Data Tools group, 59

deleting rows, duplicating worksheets, 52

Dialog Box Launcher button, 8, 15, 83

dialogs, 1, 12, 15

differences, calculating, 33, 45

document icons, 2

double-click, mouse, 3

Down scroll arrow, 7

dragging

mouse, 3

sum values, 36

drop-down lists, dialogs, 12

duplicate worksheets, 47

copying sheet, 48, 55

rows

deleting, 52, 56

inserting, 51, 55

values

clearing, 49–50, 55

entering new, 53–54

E

Editing group, 49

e-mail, sharing work, 114–115, 117

E-mail command, 114

embedded charts, 85

entry selection areas, 31

equal sign (=), formulas, 45

Excel 2007, 1

appearance, 14

changing view, 6

dialog, 12, 15

exiting, 13

interface elements, 5

menus, 10–11, 15

mouse, 3, 14

Ribbon, 8–9, 15

index

scroll bars, 7

starting, 4

terms, 2

Excel Options button, 19

Excel Options dialog, 19

F

Fehily, Chris, 2

fill handles, cell content copying, 40–42, 45

Font group, 78

fonts, formatting worksheets, 68–69, 82

footers, sharing work, 107, 116

Format Cells dialog, 82

Format Data Label dialog, 96

Format Selection button, 96

Format Text button, 110

formatting worksheets, 67

    alignment, 75, 84

    borders, 77–78, 84

    column widths, 73–74, 83

    percentages, 72

    shading, 79, 84

    text

        changing colors, 80

        fonts, 68–69, 82

        indent, 76

    tips, 81

    values, 70–71, 83

formulas

    bar, 5, 14

    Copy and Paste commands, 39

    copying, 38

    sum values, 35

    worksheet information, 26

function tooltips, 35

G

Garamond font, 69

groups, Ribbon, 8

H

Header dialog, 108

Header/Footer option (Page Setup dialog), 104

Header/Footer tab, 107

headers, sharing work, 108–110, 116

Hide Rows command, 86

horizontal scroll bar, 7

I

icons, 2

Increase Decimal button, 72

Increase Indent button, 76

Increase Indent shortcut keys, 84

indented text, formatting worksheets, 76

Insert File Name button, 109

Insert options button, 51

interface elements, 1
    Microsoft Excel 2007, 5

L

labels, worksheet information, 26

Left scroll arrow, 7

legends, charts, 92, 99

Location group, Move Chart button, 88

M

margins, adjusting, 106

Margins options (Page Setup dialog), 104

Margins tab, 108

menus, 1, 10–11, 15

Microsoft Excel 2007, 1
    appearance, 14
    changing view, 6
    dialog, 12, 15
    exiting, 13, 15
    interface elements, 5
    menus, 10–11, 15
    mouse, 3, 14
    Ribbon, 8–9, 15
    scroll bars, 7
    starting, 4
    terms, 2

Microsoft Office button, 5

Microsoft Office menus, 10

Microsoft Windows Vista: Visual QuickStart Guide, 2

mouse, 3, 14

Move Chart button, 88

Move Chart dialog, 88

N

naming, budget worksheets, 24, 44

net incomes, calculating, 37

New command, creating workbook files, 18

New shortcut key, 22

New Workbook dialog, 18

Normal view, 6

Number group
    Accounting Number Format button, 71
    Comma Style button, 70
    Increase Decimal button, 72
    Percent Style button, 72

numbers, formatting worksheets, 72

O

options buttons, dialogs, 12

Outside End command, 95

P

Page Break Preview, 6

Page Layout tab, 104

index

Page Layout view, 6
    switching to, 102
Page options (Page Setup dialog), 104
Page Setup dialog, 104–105, 108
Page Setup group, 104
Paste button, 39
Paste command, formulas, 39
Paste Options button, 39
Paste shortcut keys, 46
percent differences, calculating,
    34, 45, 64–65
Percent Style button, 72
Percent Style shortcut keys, 84
percentages, formatting worksheets, 72
pie charts, exploding, 93–94, 99
pointing mouse, 3
Print button, 112
Print command, 101
Print Preview feature, 101, 112
printing, sharing work, 113, 117
program icons, 2
push buttons, dialogs, 12

Q

Quick Access toolbar, 5, 22

R

Reference boxes, 60
references, budget worksheets, 25
resolution, computer screens, 15
Ribbon, 1, 5
    appearance of Excel 2007, 14
    Microsoft Excel 2007, 8–9, 15
right-click, mouse, 3
Right scroll arrow, 7
rollers, mouse, 14
rows
    budget worksheets, 23
    charts, hiding, 86
    duplicating worksheets
        deleting, 52, 56
        inserting, 51, 55
    headings, 5, 28
    worksheet references, 25

S

Save As dialog, 21–22
Save As shortcut key, 22
Save button, saving work, 22
Save shortcut keys, 22, 46, 56, 84
saving, workbook files, 21, 22
screens, resolution, 15

ScreenTip boxes, 8
   format, 15
   shortcut keys, 16
scroll bars, 5, 7
scroll boxes, 7
scrolling lists, dialogs, 12
Select All button, 69
Setup button, 112
shading, formatting worksheets, 79, 84
sharing work, 101
   adjusting margins, 106
   custom headers, 108–110, 116
   e-mail, 114–115, 117
   footers, 107, 116
   Page Setup dialog, 104
   Print Preview feature, 112
   printing, 113, 117
   save settings, 111, 116
   setting page options, 105, 116
   sheet selection, 103
   switching to Page Layout view, 102
Sheet option (Page Setup dialog), 104
sheet tabs, 5, 24
sheets
   duplicating, 48, 55
   workbook files, 17
shortcut keys, 22
   Bold, 84
   Clear Contents, 56

Copy, 46
Increase Indent, 84
New, 22
Paste, 46
Percent Style, 84
Save, 22, 46, 56, 84
Save As, 22
ScreenTip box, 16
Show formula bar check box, 20
Show Legend at Bottom command, 92
source worksheets, 63
Start menu, appearance, 14
status bars, 5
submenus, 11
SUM function, values, 35–36, 45
summary worksheets, 57
   Consolidation dialog, 59–62
   sheet preparation, 58
symbols
   currency
      entering values, 44
      formatting worksheets, 71
   entering values, 44

T

tabs
   dialogs, 12
   Ribbon, 8

index

text
  charts, 98, 100
  formatting worksheets
    changing colors, 80
    fonts, 68–69
    indenting, 76
text boxes, 9, 12
three-button mouse, 14
title bars, 5
titles, charts, 90–91, 99
tools, 9
Top and Bottom Border command, 77
type and drag, sum values, 36

U

Up scroll arrow, 7

V

values
  changing, 43, 46
  duplicating worksheets
    clearing, 49–50, 55
    entering new, 53–54
  entering, 31–32, 44
  formatting worksheets, 70–71, 83
  SUM function, 35–36, 45
  worksheet information, 26
vertical scroll bar, 7
View buttons, 5–6

views, changing, 6

W-X-Y-Z

windows, scroll bars, 7
Windows Control Panel, 15
Windows Explorer, 2
Windows Vista, Microsoft Excel 2007 compatibility, 1
Windows XP, Microsoft Excel 2007 compatibility, 1
Windows XP: Visual QuickStart Guide, 2
workbook files, 17
  charts, 85
    adding titles, 90–91, 99
    creating chart sheets, 88–89
    data labels, 95–97, 100
    exploding pie, 93–94, 99
    formatting text, 98, 100
    hiding row, 86
    inserting, 87, 99
    moving legends, 92, 99
  creating, 18, 22
  display options, 19–20
  saving, 21–22
Workbook Views group, 6, 102
worksheets, 17
  budget, 23
    activating cells, 27, 44
    AutoComplete rows, 44
    changing values, 43, 46

column headings, 29

Copy and Paste commands, 39, 45

copying formulas, 38

difference calculations, 33, 45

entering information, 26

fill handles, 40–42, 46

making columns wider, 30, 44

naming, 24, 44

net income calculations, 37

percent difference calculations, 34, 45

references, 25

row headings, 28

SUM function, 35–36, 45

values, 31–32, 44

consolidating, 57, 65

calculating percent differences, 64–65

checking, 63

Consolidate dialog, 59–62

sheet preparation, 58

duplicating, 47

clearing values, 49–50, 55

copying sheet, 48, 55

deleting rows, 52, 56

entering new values, 53–54

inserting rows, 51, 55

formatting, 67

alignment, 75, 84

borders, 77–78, 84

changing text colors, 80

column widths, 73–74, 83

fonts, 68–69, 82

indent text, 76

percentages, 72

shading, 79, 84

tips, 81

values, 70–71, 83

sharing work, 101

adjusting margins, 106

custom headers, 108–110, 116

e-mail, 114–115, 117

footers, 107, 116

Page Setup dialog, 104

Print Preview feature, 112

printing, 113, 117

save settings, 111, 116

setting page options, 105, 116

sheet selection, 103

switching to Page Layout view, 102

windows, 5

DATE DUE